Considering Conservation

Oceans Under Threat

Philip Neal

Dryad Press London

Contents

Introduction   3
Planet Ocean   4
Holidays by the Sea   6
Finding the Way   8
The Ocean Currents   10
Tides   12
Plankton   14
Fishing   16
Fishing Methods   18
Farming the Seas   20
Krill   22
Squid   24
Whales   26
Facts, Figures and Fantasy   28
Dolphins   30
Jellyfish – Floating Free   32
The Ocean Dustbin   34
Oil Pollution   36

Oil Disaster – *The Exxon Valdez*   38
Dumping Sewage in the Sea   40
Carry on Dumping   42
Marine Incineration of Waste   44
Nuclear Waste   46
Power from the Seas   48
Ideas for Power   50
The Oceans and the Greenhouse
    Effect   52
Down Below in Davy Jones's Locker   54
Mining the Ocean Bed   56
Political Considerations   58
Can you help?   60
Glossary   61
Resources List   62
Useful Addresses   63
Index   64

Acknowledgments

The author wishes to thank the following for their help in the preparation of this book. Queano Coletta (World Bank), Dolci Faii Guiditta (Food and Agriculture Organization of the United Nations), Rita Neal, Colin Pelton (Marine Advisory and Information Service), Paul Rodhouse (British Antarctic Survey), Shirley Singer (Ormat Turbines Ltd), Dr K. Steinkamp (Preussag).

The author and the publisher thank the following for their permission to reproduce photographs: Food and Agriculture Organization of the UN: pages 6, 16, 19, 27; World Bank: 17 (left), 18, 24, 25, 36 (top); Preussag: 57; Associated Press: 9 (top), 38, 39; Marine Information and Advisory Service, Institute of Oceanographic Sciences, Deacon Laboratory: title page, 54, 55 (top and bottom left); *Daily Telegraph*: cartoon by JAK, page 53; UK Nirex: 46; Swedish Nuclear Fuel and Waste Management Co: 47 (top); Beckett Press: 3, 36 (bottom), 37 (top right); Felix Rosenstiels widow and Son Ltd: 7 (bottom left); Norwave: 49 (top left and top right), 50; Ormat Turbines Ltd: 49 (bottom).

The diagrams and illustrations on pages 5, 13 (bottom left), 15, 16, 21, 22, 23, 25, 29, 31 (bottom), 33, 35, 45, 47, 51, 55, 56, 59 and 60 are by Sue Prince, the graph on page 20 is from the *Fish Trader* Magazine. All other maps, diagrams and photographs are those of the author.

Cover illustrations

Top: Supertankers: a convenient way to transport oil in bulk, but bringing the ever-present danger of major oil leakage (courtesy ESSO); *Centre:* oil spillage in Alaska (courtesy Frank Spooner Pictures); *Below left:* oil pollition from *Exxon Valdez* (courtesy Frank Spooner Pictures); *Below right:* Sperm Whale, Narwhal and Blue Whale (author's illustration).

Typeset by Tek-Art Ltd, Kent
and printed by
Courier International,
Tiptree, Essex
for the Publishers
Dryad Press
4 Fitzhardinge Street
London W1H 0AH

ISBN 0 7134 6372 4

Introduction

PLANET OCEAN would be a much better name than PLANET EARTH. Why? . . . because three quarters of the world's surface is water and not land. The oceans are vast, yet we see little of them – some people never see the sea in the whole of their lives. As a result we tend to treat them as everlasting and unchanging – no matter what we do. We take the oceans for granted, whilst they bathe the entire planet with their artery like currents and their freshwater extensions.

We use them for our food, we extract salt from them, we seek minerals and oil from their beds, we travel on them, we use them to transport our goods . . . we dump our rubbish into them, we disturb their floors with our mining, we pour polluted water into them from our rivers, we create accidents which contaminate them with oil and poisons . . . and yet all the while we rely on them to perpetuate the water cycle and to control the extremes of our climate.

There are danger signs that we must stop abusing the oceans. Dead and deformed creatures indicate that all is not well with the sea. Oil spillages swept up on to the shore tell a similar story – but still the oceans continue to tolerate us and supply much of our needs.

This book describes some of the amazing things about our oceans and of many things we still need to know about them: much of the ocean bed is unexplored: many mysteries remain, some simple, some intricate. It also tells the story of how we, the people of the world, are damaging our seas and what – at last – the governments of the world are starting to do on our behalf.

However, the efforts being made to CONSERVE the resources of our seas are, as yet, ONLY A DROP IN THE OCEAN!

In the UK the Royal National Lifeboat Institution organizes the lifeboat service around the British coasts. The boats are manned by volunteers.

Planet Ocean

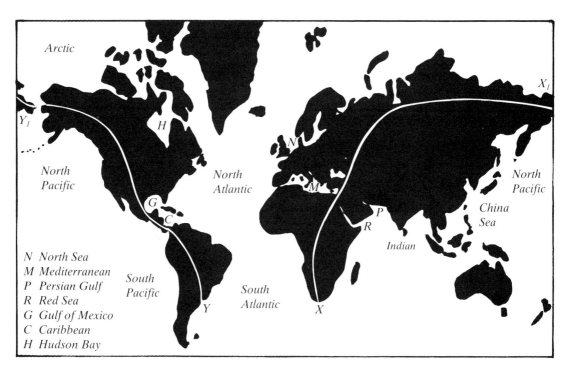

"Land" map of the world. *Antarctica is not shown on this map.*

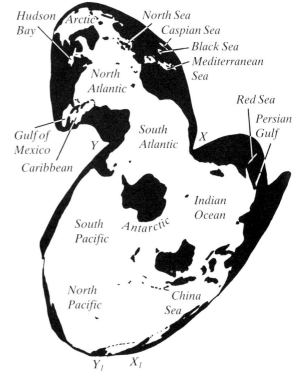

"Ocean" map of the world. *The world is a sphere. It is impossible to open out a round object and make it lie flat on a piece of paper. Cartographers (people who draw maps) have to do the best they can with their map projections. Maps of the world in our atlases are usually split through the Pacific Ocean – this enables the land mass of America to appear to the left of the map and that of Europe, Africa, Asia and Australasia to the right. The "Land" map (above) is quite a normal one where the left-hand side links up with the right-hand side. The "Ocean" map (right) has been drawn by splitting the world along the line X to Y and opening it out like the skin of an orange. Points X, Y, X1 and Y1 are marked on both maps to help you understand what has happened. Look at a globe of the world in order to understand the Ocean map properly.*

By splitting the map in this way it is possible to show the oceans as one continuous area of water. It shows Planet Earth to be a huge mass of water surrounded by land. Perhaps Planet Ocean is the better name.

This is another map projection which gives the idea of a round world. This time Antarctica is shown.

A₁   Gulf Stream
A₁₁   North Atlantic Drift
B   North Equatorial
C   Brazil
D   Kuro Siwo
E   Equatorial
F   Indian
G   East Australian
H   South Equatorial
I   North Pacific

a   Labrador
b   Canaries
c   Benguela
d   West Wind Drift
e   Peru
f   California
g   Bering
h   West Australia
i   Cape Horn

Weather forecast areas around Britain.

The seas around the British Isles are divided into areas for weather forecast purposes.

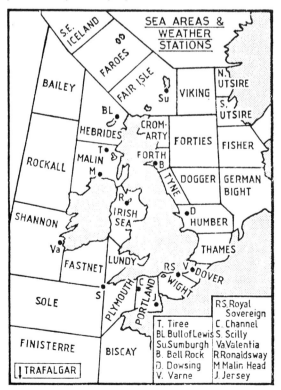

The Ocean Currents. *Currents which are warm compared with the water around them are shown in capital letters. Those which are cold are shown by small letters.*

The Water (or Hydrological) Cycle.

Most of the world's water is stored in the oceans (97.2 per cent).

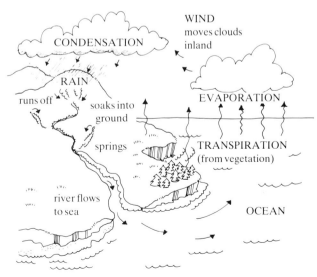

5

Holidays by the Sea

Going to the seaside is the nearest most of us get to the oceans of the world – and all we can see there is that part of the ocean waters that is in contact with the land. It is here that inshore fishermen go about their business, where holiday makers bask in the sun, swim in the sea and relax. A leisure industry has grown up around the seaside holiday, which started a hundred years ago in Victorian times. Make a list for yourself of the people who make a living from the seaside holiday, from ice cream vendors to hotel owners, from boat hirers to deck chair attendants.

Sand Dune Fixation. Planting of shrubs and marram grass binds the sand together and prevents dune movement. Cape Verde Islands in the Atlantic Ocean off West Africa.

The rocks that make up the shoreline determine the kind of beach to be found, and the slope of the land decides just how much will be available for playing on at low tide. Soft rocks, especially sandstone, will result in sandy beaches, while hard rocks or soft rocks containing hard lumps (chalk with flints in it) will mean cliffs and pebble beaches with rock pools at low tide. A gently sloping shore will mean plenty of exposed foreshore at low tide – except in tideless seas such as the Mediterranean.

Improved transport, especially the motor car and plane, has meant that people can reach the sea shore quite easily in large numbers. The pleasant places become over used, there is a need for toilet facilities with the consequent need for sewage treatment, and the beaches themselves become eroded by the traffic of many people. Protective vegetation may be worn away so badly that the sand of the dunes begins to spread. A problem of conservation arises. Positive steps have to be taken to control the situation, usually by a variety of methods which includes the planting of marram grass whose deep roots fix the sand in position. Mobile homes and caravans occupy the nearby fields and, together with camp sites and car parks obliterate the scenery which people have come to see. Holidaymakers scare away the sea birds and beach loving creatures and destroy the special plants which love these salty conditions.

In the popular resorts of the Mediterranean and other foreign seaside areas, restrictions on building are less severe than in the UK. As a result, hotels and leisure centres are built on the beautiful beaches. They do provide a fairly inexpensive place for people to enjoy themselves, but the peaceful atmosphere is ruined, the views are spoilt and often the existence of rare creatures is threatened. Turtles are a good example. In some places like Cyprus and Malaysia, turtle reserves are established in order to encourage these extraordinary creatures to breed. Turtle protection is but one example of seashore conservation by establishing nature reserves.

The coastlands of the USA and Britain have many such reserves. For example, the pelicans

Relaxation on the Seashore, Eastbourne.

off the Californian coast enjoy specially protected areas and in England the migratory sea birds are able to stop over on the nature reserve of Lindisfarne Island off the coast of Northumbria. In these areas the interested holiday tourist may visit, but under strictly controlled conditions, with some areas completely barred to their access.

The ever-widening scope of the package holiday with people going greater distances to more and more remote places, many of them seashore or island locations, threatens the natural world of the ocean edge increasingly every year. The destruction of the coral reef and the mangrove lined shore are two of the most recent problems to emerge. Yet tourism provides the money to raise local living standards, an economic factor against which it is difficult to argue.

Sea Bathing from Bathing Machines.
About 100 years ago bathing huts were moved in and out with the tide. It was considered impolite to be on the beach in swimming costumes. The sea was called the briny (brine is salt water).

Finding the Way

The seas of the world have no signposts and no traffic lights. Ships' captains have to navigate their vessels by the use of compass and maps, with the assistance of radar. Some parts of the oceans are so busy that boats have to keep to shipping lanes, "paths" across the seas traversed by one ship after another. Crowded narrow seas, such as the English Channel, need as much lane discipline with ships moving from one place to another as with vehicles on the roads . . . and boats have no brakes! Coastguards plot their movements and especially keep a wary eye open for the huge oil tankers which cannot change course easily. The skill of the captain is helped by the services of a local pilot when entering or leaving port.

The Royal Sovereign light. *Lightships have been anchored around our coasts to mark sand banks and other shallow waters. They are being replaced by light platforms similar to oil rigs. Helicopters can land on them. They also act as weather stations. This is the Royal Sovereign light in the English Channel off Hastings (see weather forecast map on page 5). They are operated by an organization known as Trinity House.*

The Corinth canal. *Some of the seas of the world are separated from each other by a narrow strip of land. Cutting through saves many days of travel. The Panama (Atlantic/Pacific connection) and the Suez (Mediterranean/Red Sea) canals are the best known. Perhaps the oldest is the Corinth canal of southern Greece – all dug without machinery!*

Road travel may be difficult but at least the surface of the road stays still and does not suddenly become rough with huge waves making driving difficult. Storms may blow ships off course and may make it dangerous for travel. The need for lighthouses and lightships, warning buoys and radio beams is essential to give due heed to the rocks which break through the waves, the sand banks which make for shallow water and the headlands which stick out to sea.

Much ocean traffic is over fairly short distances and is known as ferry traffic. The routes from Dover to Calais, from Newhaven to Dieppe and from Harwich to the Hook of Holland are but some of the links between Britain and continental Europe. Conventional boats are used, although most of them now have a 'roll-on roll-off' design. Ro-Ro boats, as they are known, are especially in demand by commercial lorries, tourist cars and coaches travelling to and from the continent. Hovercraft and hydrofoil craft now augment the traditional services and imitate aircraft travel by their use of flying procedures, hostesses and pilots.

All of this ocean traffic gives rise to problems of pollution. Despite strict international rules, ships still discharge oil from their tanks and throw indestructible rubbish into the sea. These, as we will see, wash up on the shore to pollute the foreshore and cause damage and injury to sea birds and sea creatures.

Lighthouse. Beachy Head. *Lighthouses are built to warn ships of rocks and headlands. Their lights give out beams which can be identified so that captains know where they are. This lighthouse warns sailors of the chalk cliffs between Brighton and Hastings.*

Ferry disaster, 7 March 1987. *The* Herald of Free Enterprise *sailed out of Zeebrugge harbour in Belgium, bound for Dover. The car loading doors at the front were open and let in so much sea water that the ship turned over on its side, with great loss of life. Rescue tugs are moored alongside the stricken vessel, which also contained lorries loaded with toxic chemicals which floated away into the sea.*

Ships are valuable and carry valuable cargoes. They have to be insured. It is necessary to know where a ship is all the time. Most of this is controlled by Lloyds of London – although each ship has to be registered by a single country, to come under their rules and to fly their flag. Some companies register their ships with small countries because they have less rigid rules concerning safety and the welfare of crews: this saves money for the owners. Where ships are registered in such a way they need to fly the flag of that country: it is known as a "flag of convenience".

Yet, despite all of the hazards of ocean travel, it remains the best way of moving heavy goods over long distances. Every time you eat New Zealand lamb, Jamaican bananas or Californian plums try to remember that they have probably travelled on the world's oceans to your table, often in specially constructed refrigerated or temperature-controlled ships. Air travel may have replaced ocean travel for people, but for goods – despite an increase in air transportation – carriage by ship is still the main way.

The Ocean Currents

The life blood of your body is carried by arteries to all parts, driven by the pumping of your heart. The waters of the sea are carried to all parts of the oceans by currents driven by the winds, which are driven by the heat of the sun. Add to this the effects of the tides and the spin of the earth and you have the cause of about 20 major surface current movements, some of which are of warm water and some of cold (see map page 11).

The ocean currents can be compared with our arteries: certainly, the water they carry is as important to the life of Planet Earth as is the blood of the human body. Huge masses of water are transported over vast distances: moving the cold waters of the polar regions towards the tropics and the warm water of these equatorial regions north and south to Arctica and Antarctica. As they come up against the land

they have an influence on the climate which can alter the whole ecosystem – that is to say, the sort of plants and animals which can live there and the way that people also live. How hot or cold, how wet or dry, how cloudy or clear, how windy or calm, all result in part from the ocean currents affecting that part of the world. They carry with them the plants and creatures of the plankton and of other nutritious matter dragged up from the ocean deep by wind and current. With food in abundance, fish and other marine animals gather together where the current brings the food harvest: this creates rich fishing grounds.

The ocean currents also transport undesirable matter. Pollution carried by air alone is not enough to explain that the fat of Antarctic penguins contains traces of pesticides used only in places very far from the South Pole. The poisons must have been carried there in the sea, and these include the infamous DDT. Oil spillage is also transported by ocean current so that far away from the source of oil pollution the sea surface is covered with the brown or black tar of crude oil. How long before the easterly turn of the warm ocean current, the Kiro Siwo,

Flotsam on the Beach. *Much of the debris on the beach is refuse thrown over the side of ships and moved across the oceans by the currents. These are plastic bottles found on the South Coast of England. French language labelling means that they have crossed the English Channel at least.*

Breakwaters. *Ocean currents reach the shore, their surfaces disturbed by the wind to form waves. The power of these crashing waves is such that strong breakswaters have to be built to reduce the force of the water. They also reduce "longshore drift", where the sand and pebbles are moved along the shore. One side of the breakwater has a beach higher than the other, showing how the obstruction prevents the pebbles moving along.*

Repairs can be made only at low tide.

carries the oil of *Exxon Valdez* (page 38) across the North Pacific to the Asian coast?

One interesting seaside investigation is to examine the flotsam along the shoreline – but do take care, as some dangerous objects can be washed ashore – for instance, explosive mines left over from the Second World War, and drums of chemicals from shipwrecks. Never, open a bottle or canister containing any material or, more especially, touch anything that might be an explosive device. Many items such as plastic bottles or packing cases will have writing on them, possibly even the place where they were made. If you can identify the language you are part of the way to solving where they came from.

The Gulf Stream Drift and the Sargasso Sea.

Do you have a record player? Instead of a disc, put on a sheet of paper. Draw a straight line from the centre to the outside. Now start the turntable. While it is moving, try to draw a straight line from the middle to the edge. Look at the result. The line will be curved and deflected to one side. The effect is similar with the winds and ocean currents of the world. As they try to blow or flow in one direction they are deflected by the spin of the earth to the right in the Northern Hemisphere, or to the left in the South. This is called the Coriolis Effect. *With the water the friction of the flow against the rest of the water causes the lower layers to be deflected more than the top. In the end, the effect of friction plus that of Coriolis means that the water moves at right-angles to the wind. This is called the Ekman Flow.*

This map shows how these forces combine to create an area of water in the North Atlantic known as the Sargasso Sea and squeeze a flow from the Gulf of Mexico to North Europe. This is the Gulf Stream Drift, which is estimated to have five times the amount of water flowing in it as is in ALL the rivers of the world.

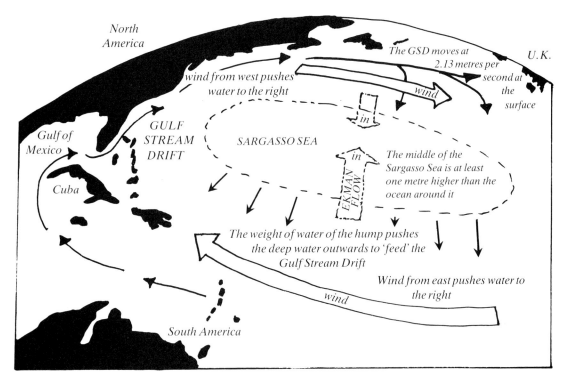

Tides

"Time and tide wait for no man!". Have you heard this proverb? It simply means that there is nothing at all that can be done to prevent time moving on, or the tides of the oceans rising and falling. Almost a thousand years ago King Canute is said to have proved this when, in order to show his ministers that even a king was powerless to alter this great force of nature, he unsuccessfully commanded the tide to go back.

Unlike solid rock, water moves easily: the gravitational pull of the moon and the sun makes the ocean surface rise and fall as shown in the diagram. As far as we are concerned the result is that the tide comes in (it flows) and it goes out (it ebbs). This means that the sea water moves up the shore and then returns down it.

High and low tide at Saundersfoot, South Wales.
Are you able to recognize the same boats afloat at high tide and, about six hours later, on the mud at low tide?

How much land is covered at high tide and how much is revealed at low tide depends on the amount of rise and fall of the water and, very importantly, on how steeply the land slopes down to the sea. A steep slope will result in little forward and backward movement. A gentle slope will lead to the tide exposing a great deal of the sea bottom at low tide.

The tidal cycle, twice from high tide through low tide back to high tide, takes almost 26 hours. This is the time it takes the moon to return to the same part of the sky after the world has revolved once. The full cycle happens twice because high water occurs both when the moon is directly overhead and when it is exactly on the opposite side of the world. Thus high tides rise twice a day at almost 13-hour intervals, with, for example, high tide on Monday at noon being followed by another high tide about 45 minutes after midnight and a further high tide on Tuesday, just before one-thirty in the afternoon.

Sometimes high water reaches a particular place by two routes, for example at Southampton – where the Isle of Wight blocks the entrance to Southampton Water. One high tide reaches the port at one time, and another, which has travelled around the other side of the island, arrives sometime later. Southampton has a "double tide". Other places have restricted access, preventing a tidal flow. The Mediterranean Sea is like this – it has no tides at all. One result of this is that the beaches of Mediterranean holiday resorts do not receive a twice daily wash – as with other places in the world. Tidal movement also helps to remove sewage, oil and other pollutants, although in practice the tide may simply move the pollutants farther along the coast.

River estuaries form a funnel. As the high tide moves into the estuary, the restricted size means that the water level rise is very exaggerated. The Severn Estuary in the UK and the Bay of Fundy in Canada have the highest tidal ranges in the world. (The tidal range is the difference in height between high and low water.)

One problem with some ports is that at low tide the water is too shallow for boats to remain afloat. It means that either boats cannot remain at low tide, or the docks have to have lock gates to keep the water trapped and so remain at a high level. With this system large ships can only enter or leave dock at high tide. This places a great restriction on the times when the docking of a ship is possible.

If it is possible to trap the water of the high tide behind a lock gate it is also possible to trap it behind a barrage across the estuary. The water can be allowed to escape at low tide via a turbine. This will create electricity, as you can see on page 50.

The gravitational pull of the sun and moon on the oceans of the world.
A and B give the highest tides.
C gives the lowest high tides.

A

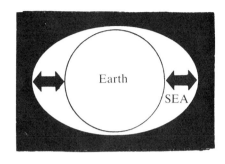

A   Sun and moon in line on same side

B

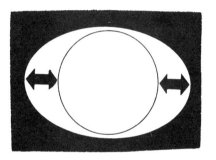

B   Sun and moon in line but on opposite sides

C

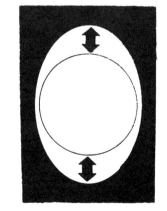

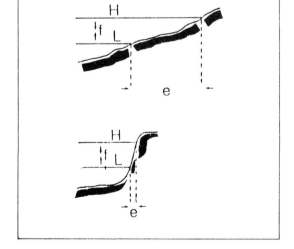

The effect of the slope of the shore.
The fall (f) between High (H) and Low (L) tide is the same but the area of exposed beach (e) is much greater where the slope is gentle than where it is steep.

C   Sun and moon at right angles

Plankton

When we think about farming and food production, we normally think about fields. Fields are the places where crops grow to be harvested or eaten by the farm animals. The oceans of the world do not have any "fields" but they do have large areas covered with plants which are "grazed" by animals, which are themselves eaten by other creatures. The plants gather food from the nutrients carried by the water and, unlike the land plants, they are free to move from place to place as the currents carry them about the ocean. In fact their name PHYTOPLANKTON means "drifting plants" in the Greek language.

These plants are very small, so much so that as many as 200,000 may be found in a cubic metre of sea water. As with land plants, the phytoplankton exploit the energy of the sun through the process of photosynthesis, taking in carbon dioxide and emitting oxygen. They are a most important factor in the reduction of CO^2 in the atmosphere, which helps to combat the Greenhouse Effect (see page 52). The plants are concentrated in the top 100 metres of the sea – the depth to which sunlight penetrates.

As this plant life relies on biologically rich areas, it is most likely to be found in masses near to the coasts, where nutrients are brought down by rivers or at places where turbulence in the sea water forces material up from the seabed. This happens where ocean currents meet.

It follows, therefore, that around the British Isles and Iceland, for example, the seas are rich in plankton and that in the North Atlantic, where the warm waters of the Gulf Stream Drift meet the cold waters of the Newfoundland Current, further areas of plankton concentrations (known as BLOOMS) are found. It also follows that areas of richness are matched by areas of sparcity. In other words, the oceans of the world have their equivalent to the deserts

The ocean grazing "fields".
The black zones are areas where phytoplankton growth is heavy or moderately heavy. The rippled areas have little plankton growth.

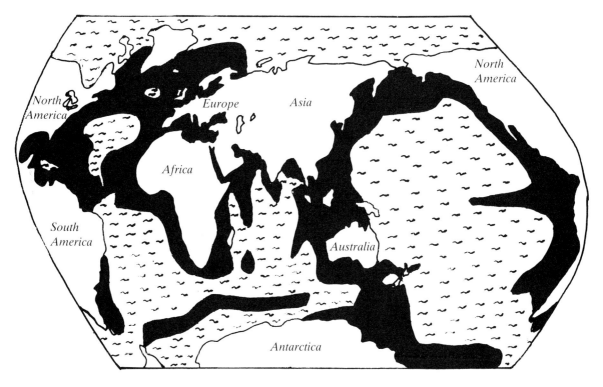

and rainforests on dry land. It is even possible to see these by the variations of sea colour as observed by satellites.

It is on the phytoplankton plants that small sea creatures feed. These are known as the ZOOPLANKTON, consisting of minute animals such as COPEPODS and larger (though still small) shrimps and shrimplike creatures as are described in the next pages. As well as these, there are the larvae of most fish and shellfish. It is believed that copepods are the most numerous of all the animals found on earth.

Carnivores amongst the zooplankton feed on other small creatures but they and their prey provide the food for small fish, squid and jellyfish as well as for sea birds, penguins, seals and other bigger animals. Incredibly, one of the largest of all animals is sustained by zooplankton – as we shall see later.

Small fish such as the anchovy, herring and sardine eat the animals of the zooplankton and they themselves are the food of the larger fish of the oceans and seas. We eat the fish to complete the food chain.

We also poison the plankton by sending into the seas our waste and washouts from our fields and factories. For example, DDT still persists as a poison despite the fact that it has been used sparingly for the last few years. One estimate is that one million of the one-and-a-half million tonnes of this powerful insect killer produced before 1970 is to be found in ocean sediments, from where it is still being transferred into the tissues of plankton and so on up the food chain into our bodies.

More recently Polychlorinated Biphenyls (PCBs) have been introduced into manufacturing processes, particularly for electrical and heating equipment and for paints, plastics and paper making. PCBs are known to have a disastrous effect on animals, causing illness and death. Zooplankton, shrimps, crab larvae, the young of shellfish and even adult fish, are killed by PCBs. It is also quite possible that the presence of these chemicals can cause large sea mammals, such as sea lions, to abort their young (that is they are born too early to survive).

Samples of plankton taken in the mid 1970s in the estuary of Canada's huge St Lawrence River showed that they contained 93,000 parts of PCB per million. *Five parts per million are rated as an acceptable limit!* If we permit the plankton of the seas to be poisoned we are, in effect, poisoning ourselves – a frightening thought.

Phytoplankton. Under the microscope the large variety of plants of different shapes and sizes are shown to exist in a small amount of seawater.

Fishing

I suppose it is because we live on an island surrounded by the sea that fish (and chip) shops are found in such profusion: there are over 9000 of these shops in the UK. If you just ask for "fish and chips, please" you will be sold cod as the fish. This shows how common this fish specie has been – but this is no longer the case. Overfishing (catching too many fish) has led countries such as Iceland to protect their fish stocks: after what was known as the "Cod War" of the 1970s, foreign boats, most of them British, were banned from trawling closer than 100 miles to the Icelandic shore. As a result, fishing ports like Grimsby are no longer busy

Unloading a catch of shrimps in Panama.

harbours for deep sea fishing boats and much of the cod we eat is brought to us by Icelandic boats.

The cold slabs of the fishmongers shop are interesting places to look at. Round fish, flat fish and shellfish indicate that each creature lives in a different part of the sea, where it is able to find its own type of food. There are six main sorts of sea creatures which are hunted for our food supplies. They are –

1 **Pelagic fish** They live near the surface of the sea, feeding either on plankton or attacking each other. They range in size from the fairly small mackerel, herring and anchovy to large fish such as tuna and shark.

2 **Demersal fish** They live near to or on the bottom of the sea. In order to blend in with the seabed many of these species have evolved into

Shark are caught in Sport Fishing.
Large fish have to be "gaffed" in order to be hauled aboard a boat. Mako Shark – about 1800 mm long.

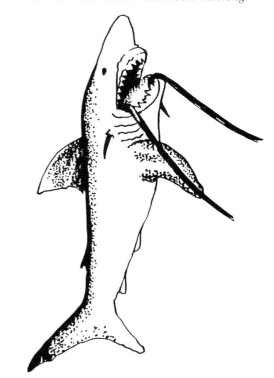

flat fish, e.g. sole and plaice. Much of the food which they consume is detritus (waste) which falls to the bottom.

3 **Shellfish** These include crabs and shrimps. Most live fairly near to the shore, eating particles of food in the water or preying on smaller creatures.

4 **Cephalopods** These are the octopus and squid. They are not very popular as food in the UK but in other countries they are in great favour.

5 **Mammals** Whales and dolphins are two of the sea mammals – they give birth to live young. Whales are such large animals that catching only a few provides as much food as hauling in many netfuls of fish.

6. **Reptiles** Turtles, for example, are accepted as a delicacy in many countries.

There are many ways of catching fish, depending on the type of fish being hunted and

Cod fish recognized by the "whisker" on the jaw.

Canning mackerel at the Alpesca Plant in Mar del Plata, Argentina.

the location of the fishing areas. Inshore, that is near to the coast line, small boats use lines with baited hooks, nets, or various types of basket traps for lobsters and crabs. Inshore fishing is important, particularly where fishermen supply holiday resorts, but it is the deep-sea commercial fishing, where boats are away from their home port for days or weeks, which is the mainstay of the industry. Fish not wanted for human consumption, or fish which are unsuitable for eating, are turned into fertilizer, pet food or fish oil. If boats catch only for fertilizer production this is known as "Industrial Fishing".

Sea fishing is very wasteful. Sea creatures which are unwanted are caught and not used. The natural food chain is disturbed unnecessarily. For every tonne of prawns caught it is estimated that three tonnes of other fish are killed and thrown away. The massive drift or "gill" nets are often left to drift overnight and are then retrieved. In the Pacific Ocean they are used to catch squid and tuna but the small-mesh nylon nets snare, and usually kill, almost all marine life – dolphin, sea birds, whales and turtles. Conservationists call them "the Wall of Death". The demand for a global ban on drift – net fishing is growing with the South Pacific Forum of 15 nations heading the pressure. It is estimated that 20,000 porpoises die every year in salmon nets in the North Atlantic.

Tropical fish on an English fishmonger's slab.

Fishing Methods

Demersal trawl

The net is towed along the seabed by two cables attached to the trawl boat. The mouth of the net is kept open by the thrust of the sea on two otter boards, like doors, attached to the cables. The wide net narrows down to the tail or "cod-end". Floats keep the top of the net open and rollers called "bobbins" keep the bottom on the seabed. If two boats are used one cable goes to each and it is not necessary to have otter boards.

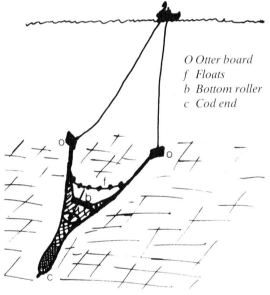

O Otter board
f Floats
b Bottom roller
c Cod end

Demersal, deep sea, trawling.

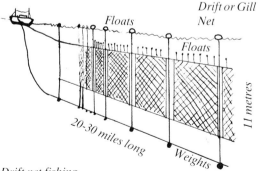

Drift or Gill Net

Floats

Floats

20-30 miles long

Weights

11 metres

Drift net fishing.
Used to catch pelagic fish. As fish cannot swim backwards they cannot escape after swimming into the net. The size of the mesh determines the size of the fish caught.

Inshore throw-net fishing.
Colombian fishermen cast the net on the water, circle round and then draw it in.

Seine net

With a seine net the fishing vessel circles around and traps fish which are on or just above the sea bed. The net is much wider than the trawl net, with a cable attached to each side. One cable is attached to a floating buoy marked by a flag. The other cable remains attached to the ship, which sails in a semi-circular course back towards the buoy. The buoy is taken on board and a winch hauls in the net. As the cables move the fish which are inside the circle are frightened into the net and on up to the cod end. Sometimes this method is called "fly-dragging".

Purse seine

A huge net often over 500 metres long and 150 metres deep is used to encircle a shoal of fish. With one end attached to a buoy the boat sails in a wide circle, returning to the buoy. The purse string is drawn tight so that the whole net has the appearance of an upturned pudding basin. The net is pulled in towards the boat and often large "vacuum" cleaners or fish pumps are used to suck the catch into the holds. The biggest nets in use would encircle a space equal to that occupied by St Paul's Cathedral.

Korean fishermen hauling in a Purse Seine net.
The seagulls indicate that there are fish in the net.

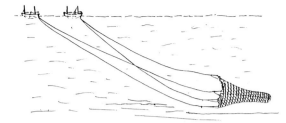

Mid water trawling.

Mid water trawl

Two boats tow a trawl net behind them. The great advantage is that the net can be used at a depth where the shoals of fish are known to be swimming, as determined by the use of echo sounding equipment.

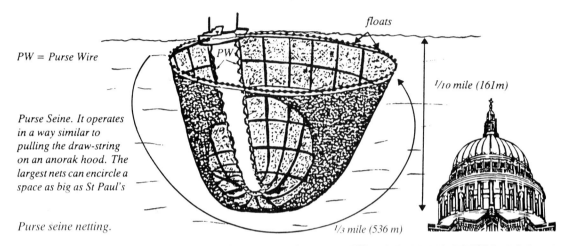

PW = Purse Wire

floats

PW

$^1/_{10}$ mile (161m)

Purse Seine. It operates in a way similar to pulling the draw-string on an anorak hood. The largest nets can encircle a space as big as St Paul's

$^1/_3$ mile (536 m)

Purse seine netting.

Farming the Seas

Sea and freshwater fishing is hunting – chasing a wild creature which may or may not be where you want it to be. Keeping fish in a pond,

A Scottish fish farm.

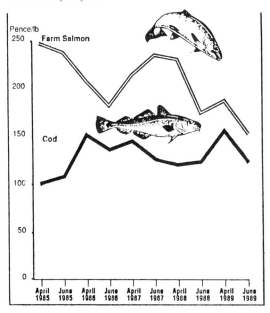

Floating fish cages do not improve the scenery, which is another disadvantage of fish farming. In 1980 there were 43 salmon farms in Scotland, in 1983 there were 100, in 1986 the number had risen to 280. From 500 tonnes of salmon in 1979, the farms are now producing 12,500 tonnes. By 1992 this is estimated to reach 50,000 tonnes. As more salmon are farmed, so the price per pound weight will fall. It becomes almost as cheap as cod.

feeding them and finally catching them for food is farming. By "farming", we mean keeping an animal in captivity so that it is where you want it, when you want it, just like keeping a herd of bullocks for their meat. Farming aquatic (water-living) animals is on the increase, especially for those which bring in a good price when sold: salmon and lobsters, for example.

Farming like this is nothing new; the Romans, Egyptians, Greeks, Japanese and, in particular, the Chinese have practised AQUACULTURE (fish farming) for thousands of years. Mostly this has been by keeping carp or trout in ponds, or often, in the case of the Chinese, stocking the flooded rice fields with fish so that they can, as it were, reap two harvests – the rice and fish. This is freshwater farming for freshwater creatures.

Sea-water farming, too, has been practised over the years – in particular the farming of shellfish, especially oysters. Now the idea of farming both fish and plants is spreading. Most of the sea inlets of Scotland have floating cages in which salmon – a most expensive fish – are reared. Similar developments are taking place in Norwegian fiords.

Any salmon which escape from either country soon meet up with the wild salmon of the northern North Sea. Unfortunately this can have a very serious effect. Salmon reared in farms are far more docile than wild salmon. It is feared that cross breeding between the "tame" and the wild salmon may produce a type of salmon which is unsuited to the rigours of the migration into the ocean and the return later (for details of this effect see *Hunting, Shooting and Fishing* in the Considering Conservation series).

Yet this is only one difficulty. The droppings from the hundreds of fish in the fish cages together with uneaten food pellets fall to the seabed. The effect is similar to spreading sewage and eutrophication takes place (for an explanation see page 42). Chemicals are used to prevent the spread of disease and of parasites. One is called Nuvan and is intended to kill sea lice; this it does but it also spreads into the surrounding waters and, it is claimed, kills off crab and lobster larvae. The diseases brought

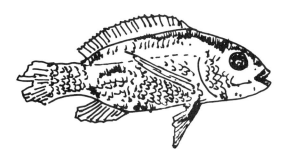

Tilapia. The East African fish species Tilapia is one of the fastest growing fish in the world. It is beginning to replace carp in fish farms. In farms near Shanghai, China three different species of carp are bred and swim through the ponds, some living on grass and other vegetation, some on plankton fertilized by the pig and duck manure and others on shellfish which live on the bottom. Each level of the pond is used.

so seaweed growing is to arable (crop) farming. China and Japan (where production is declining) farm kelp, a type of seaweed.

Yet in spite of all these examples, the use of the sea as a farm is only just beginning.

Dragging kelp from the sea.
At the Qingdao Kelp Farm in Northern China they are experimenting with different kinds of kelp, especially varieties which will grow well in southern warmer waters. China produces about 150,000 tonnes of dry kelp every year. Half is used as food and half for producing "alginates" which go to the cosmetic, food and medicine factories. Iodine is extracted from seaweed too. Shellfish, including oysters, can be farmed on kelp beds.

about by the close contact of the farmed salmon with each other can be transmitted to the wild salmon in the surrounding sea. In Norway, some infected farmed salmon were imported. The parasite known as Helminth spread into 20 rivers. The only way to eliminate the infection was to poison the rivers to kill off the parasites – and all of the wild fish which now had the parasite as well.

Fish farms attract hungry seals, herons and other wild creatures. A survey of 47 fish farms showed that 319 seals had been deliberately or accidentally killed. One estimate is that over 1000 seals, 200 herons and 2000 cormorants and shags are killed by fish farmers annually.

World wide there are farms which raise lobsters, crabs, sea cucumbers (sea slug), abalones, trout, shrimps, crayfish and many others. Many of the mussels now eaten are raised in controlled conditions. One interesting development is the farming of eels in the hot water discharge from atomic power stations, which are invariably located beside the sea.

Some extreme schemes have been put forward, such as ranching large fish. This would involve ocean "cowboys" rounding up the large fish and driving them into an enclosure to be caught. Already tunny are kept in large retaining nets in Japan's inshore sea areas, where they are fed until large enough for slaughter. There is even a scheme to rear whales in captivity which, if it was successful, would go a long way to conserve the stocks of wild whales.

As fish farming is to cattle and sheep farming,

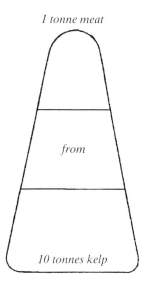

1 tonne meat

from

10 tonnes kelp

Kelp can be fed to animals instead of grass.

Krill

Sometimes people use the word "shrimp" to describe someone they consider small or unimportant. Yet in the world of the seas, shrimps and shrimp-like creatures are a vital and most important link in the chain of life. EUPHAUSIIDS are small animals similar to shrimps, pink in colour and omnivorous – able to eat animal or vegetable food. They live in water all around the world at different depths, some near to the surface and others deep down. In Antarctic waters they exist in huge numbers, some scientists estimating that the total population weighs between 300 million and 6500 thousand million tonnes, although such estimates have often proved to be inaccurate in the past. Of these, one species is known as KRILL. Each grows to about 52 mm (two inches) in length and sometimes lives crowded into swarms, so that the sea appears to be a pink colour.

Fishing fleets from the USSR, Chile and Japan, in particular, trawl in large catches of krill which are eaten direct as "shrimps" or as krill tails and even breaded krill sticks. In those three countries, together with Norway (where the word "krill" means "Whale Food"), Poland and West Germany, krill is made into paste, and added to other foods to give them an added "sea food" flavour. Still more importantly, the chemical industry can extract fat, pigment and enzymes from the krill which are then used in the manufacture of dyes, fabrics, cosmetics, adhesives, drugs and paper strengtheners. The

Krill. To the unskilled eye they look like small shrimps.

Food for the Blue Whale.
The Blue (or Baleen) Whales skim krill from the surface or gulp mouthfuls from a shoal. They close the mouth and force out water through the slats of their baleen, the filter "teeth". The krill are trapped and swallowed.

demand for this harvest from the sea is growing and though the estimated haul is put at only two shrimps in every hundred, over-fishing of other sea creatures began in a similar way.

Over exploitation of the krill stocks is a dangerous prospect, for they form a very important link in the fragile food chain of the oceans. Krill live on the phytoplankton and the smaller animals of the zooplankton, of which they are themselves a part. They filter out the very small particles of food from the ocean currents, using their front legs which are covered with fine bristles and which they position before their mouths. The next time you eat prawns or shrimps look for their bristly leg filters.

Many sea creatures live by eating krill, in particular sea birds/crabs, squid, seals and, almost unbelievably, one of the largest animals

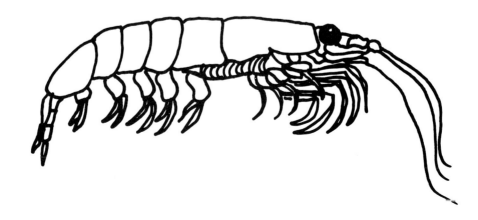

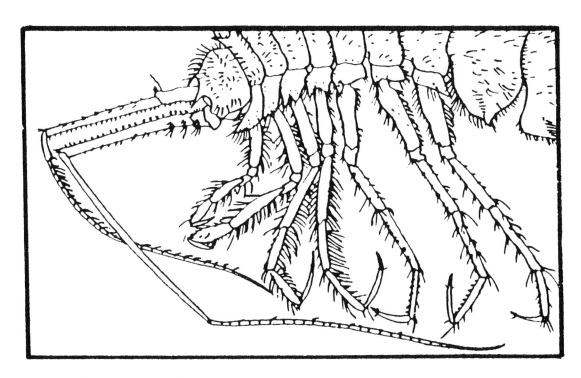

of the world, the baleen or blue whale. Every "bite" takes in nearly a tonne of krill. Whaling has depleted the number of blue whales in Antarctica so that the probable consumption of 200 million tonnes of krill every year by these whales has been reduced to about 50 million tonnes. This leaves more for other animals – to the benefit of the seal and sea birds. If fishermen continue to take more krill, will it be these "new arrivals" on the scene which will have less to eat, or will it be the already much reduced whale population? The consequences of interfering with a natural balance can never be calculated because too often the conservation considerations come too late.

The need for research into the habits of the krill is high. Little enough is known of their spawning areas and spawning habits. How quickly do they grow? How long do they live if permitted their natural span? Are the swarms, often covering areas of up to five square kilometres, to be found all the year round, or are they only seasonal? How many more are living outside the swarms? Do the krill migrate around the seas? So many questions about this lowly but vital animal need to be answered. As with the rest of the maritime world, there is so much more to be learnt.

Certainly the krill is no "shrimp" if "shrimps" are unimportant!

Filter feeders.

Krill, prawns, crabs and other shellfish filter food from the water, using the bristles on their legs as a sieve.

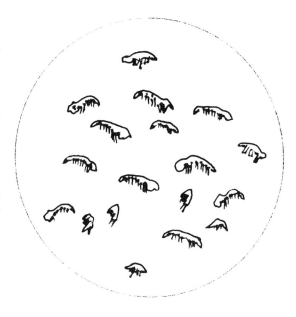

Jumping out of their skin.

When attacked krill can shed their outer case, leaving it floating behind. To a predator it still looks like a shoal of krill.

Squid

Squid are to be found in most sea areas and are common in the oceans of the South Atlantic, South Pacific and Antarctica. They are members of the family Cephalopods, to which octopus also belong. In some countries of the world they are an important fish product.

The Falkland Islands in the South Atlantic are a dependency of Britain and it was because of their invasion by Argentina that the Falklands war was fought in 1982. Argentina calls the islands the Malvinas and claims them as her territory. Squid fishing around the islands is an important source of income for the Falklanders and it was to control foreign fishing rights that the Falkland Islands Conservation Zone (FICZ) was created. All ships fishing in these waters have to be licensed.

There are two main species of squid in the Falkland waters – *Loligo Gahi*, which likes the shallower waters near to the island shores, and *Ilex Argentinus*, which prefers to live away from the land in deep water. The Loligo squids gather together in dense schools near the seabed and are caught by normal trawl methods, using large trawl nets dragged along the sea bottom.

Ilex are bigger and though they, too, swim together in schools they vary the depth at which they live. Modern ships use colour video sonar to locate these creatures. Most of the Ilex

Octopus are dried on poles in Mauritius.

fishing is carried out at night by boats which have an array of lamps around the vessel which attract the squid. Brightly coloured lures (imitation fish) called jigs are lowered by line into the water. Attached to them are barbless hooks. A modern jigging vessel is fully automated, having about 90 fishing lamps and 80 jigging machines. These lower the 2000 or more jigs straight down into the sea, where the squid attack the brightly-coloured objects and are caught on the hooks. The fishing master of the ship controls the jigging machines, using a micro computer into which is fed information about position and depth of the schools provided by the sonar equipment.

Not too much is known about the life-cycle of the squid. They seem to live for little more than a year, growing very rapidly. It appears that they spawn only once, to die soon afterwards. It is difficult to judge how many there are in the seas of the world. Numbers seem to vary annually because of the unpredictable and unexplained high death rates of some squid every year. In the Antarctic, birds, seals and whales are thought to consume 35 million tonnes every year, while Sperm whales world-wide consume 100 million tonnes annually – but like all other estimates, these are only a rough guide.

In the mid-1980s only two million tonnes of squid were being fished and although the increasing interest in them as a food for people or animals will inevitably bring about a larger catch, especially in Antarctic waters, there is still a long way to go before they are overfished. Compared with the estimated world annual catch of 80 million tonnes of cod, skate, tuna and all other kinds of fish, squid fishing is a small enterprise as yet. Nevertheless, increased interest in squid may well mean extra fishing in the Southern Ocean waters of Antarctica, as the sea around New Zealand and the Falklands is so tightly controlled. Sensible management and conservation policies are needed as well as international control of pollution, so that the problems of the Northern waters are not repeated in the south. Even now there is some evidence that oil and chemical poisons from the rest of the world are reaching Antarctica.

Children setting out squid on to drying racks in Mercedes village, Philippines. Each fish is about as long as the little boy's foot.

A handful of octopus in the fish market, Vera Cruz, Mexico.

STARFISH BY THE THOUSAND

Fishermen in the Irish Sea are complaining of the population explosion in STARFISH. Some trawlers have caught up to 50,000 of them in ONE haul of the net. There have been so many that the mesh of the net has torn apart. With their nets bulging with starfish there is little room left for the cod and other fish that are being hunted. Unfortunately for the fishermen, the starfish have no sale value. Like so many other things in the oceans it adds up to just another mystery. Obviously the Irish Sea pollution is not affecting the starfish adversely.
(The *Irish Press*, 1989)

Whales

Imagine several horses galloping along a hard surfaced road. The regular tapping noise of their hooves is said to be similar to the clicking noises coming from a school of Sperm whales as they use sound waves to hunt squid in the depths of the ocean. As the chasing whales near their target the clicks get louder and more rapid until, suddenly, they stop. The squid has been caught; only its hard "beak" will pass through the whale.

The Sperm is but one of the 80-plus species of whales. They range in size from the largest creature ever to live on earth, the Blue whale (up to 140 tonnes and 30 metres long), to the small dolphin and narwhals (under 100 kilograms and one metre in length). Sperm whales can weigh nearly 40 tonnes for a bull (male) and measure 15 metres long.

In the nineteenth century the Right whale (so called because it was the "right" one to catch), the Western Gray whale and the Humpback were hunted almost to extinction. In the twentieth century it was the turn of the Blue whale, the Fin whale, the Bowhead, the Sei whale and most recently the Minke whale to be hunted towards danger point.

There is much that we do not know about the whale family and their behaviour. Inside the head of the Sperm whale, for example, there is a large reservoir of oil, given the name of spermaceti, which may be part of its echo location and/or its diving system. The number of Sperm whales has fallen drastically in the last hundred years from over a million to a few hundred thousand today, as they have been hunted and killed for their special oil. Originally whales were hunted for their meat, fat (blubber, to be rendered down into oil), whale bone, ambergris for perfume, ink, and other by products. A single majestic 60 tonne, 25 metre living beast can, these days, be killed by explosive harpoon missiles and reduced to a pile of meat and oil within one hour inside a factory ship, such as the Japanese ship *Nisshin Maru 3*. Nowadays it is the meat, considered a luxury dish in Japan, that is sought – despite the agreed restrictions on whaling. One hopeful

Some of the whale species.

Whales are divided into those with teeth and those with baleens. The former hunt squid, tuna and smaller whales: the latter filter eat krill (see page 22). A Blue whale eats three tonnes of krill daily. The load a lorry can carry is shown somewhere on the side. Find a three tonner and imagine its full load of krill for a Blue whale's daily supply.

The elephant gives you a size comparison for each whale!

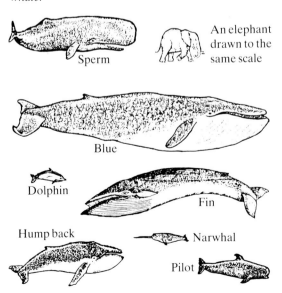

An elephant drawn to the same scale

Sperm

Blue

Dolphin

Fin

Hump back

Narwhal

Pilot

Whalebone. In Victorian times ladies wore tight, stiff corsets to produce a slim figure. They were laced up until it hurt. The shape was kept by long, thin, flexible whale bones.

development is an experiment with whale farming, which may lead to whale hunting becoming unnecessary. The plan includes collecting whale milk!

Aboriginal fishing

This title is given to the hunting of whales and other creatures by people who have such actions as part of their history: for example, the Eskimoes of Northern Canada and Greenland. Off Alaska, the Inuits hunt rare Bowhead whales except that now they use guns instead of spears and fast boats instead of canoes. Perhaps the most objectionable example is the *Faroes Grind* – the name given to the slaughter of Pilot whales by the inhabitants of the Faroe Islands to the north of Scotland. Nowadays the Faroese islanders enjoy a high standard of living and really do not need the free meat from the whales. Indeed, most of the bodies of the whales are thrown back into the sea. I find it hard to enjoy the idea of Faroese children being given the unborn Pilot whales, taken from the womb of female whales, to play with as a gruesome "toy".

International Whaling Commission

Because of the obvious question of survival of many of the whale species, an International Whaling Commission was formed in 1946: though it has no legal basis to enforce its decisions on any country, it has led to most countries of the world recognizing the problem and, as with the United Kingdom, to stop whaling altogether. Iceland, Japan and the USSR were the worst offenders in continuing to hunt for whales, but even they have reduced the killing. Japan claims that its programme of whaling is for research, a claim challenged by

The Faroes Grind. Islanders looking at the meat share out after the slaughter of Pilot whales.

conservationists. Even since the 1986 commercial ban, 11,000 whales have been slaughtered. The outlook for whales is gloomy but no longer grim. Unfortunately, scientists have no real idea how long it will take whale numbers to recover, in particular for those of the biggest species. "Save the Whale" is still an important rallying cry for environmental groups.

Jojoba

Jojoba.

The desert shrub called jojoba (*Simmondsia chinensis*) produces seeds which can be crushed to yield an oil which is similar to the oil found in the head of the Sperm whale. Sperm oil is used mainly as a special lubricant for machinery operating at high speeds. It is also used in the making of lipstick, cold cream, shaving cream, medicinal ointments, dye solvents and fixers, detergents, alcohols and various other powders and pastes. Since jojoba bushes grow in semi desert conditions, particularly in Mexico, California and Arizona in the USA and could be grown in Australia, Israel and the Sudan, it is a valuable crop for difficult agricultural areas. One Sperm whale gives about three tonnes of oil. A similar amount will come from the jojoba on two hectares (four football pitches) of land. It needs little attention whilst growing and, in particular, does not require fertilizer or pesticide. It almost seems too good to be true. I wonder why it was not exploited before the whale became endangered?

Facts, Figures and Fantasy

Of the 103 known chemical elements the sea contains 84

Oxygen	857,000	Iodine	.06	Yttrium	.0003
Hydrogen	108,000	Barium	.03	Silver	.0003
Chlorine	19,000	Indium	.02	Neon	.00014
Sodium	10,500	Zinc	.01	Cadmium	.00011
Magnesium	1,350	Iron	.01	Tungsten	.0001
Sulphur	885	Aluminum	.01	Xenon	.000052
Calcium	400	Molybdenum	.01	Selenium	.00009
Potassium	380	Nickel	.0054	Germanium	.00007
Bromine	65	Tin	.003	Chromium	.00005
Carbon	28	Copper	.003	Thorium	.00005
Strontium	8.1	Arsenic	.003	Scandium	.00004
Boron	4.6	Uranium	.003	Lead	.00003
Silicon	3.0	Vanadium	.002	Mercury	.00003
Fluorine	1.3	Manganese	.002	Gallium	.00003
Argon	.6	Krypton	.0025	Bismuth	.000017
Nitrogen	.5	Titanium	.001	Lanthanum	.000012
Lithium	.18	Cobalt	.00027	Gold	.000011
Rubidium	.12	Cesium	.0005	Thallium	.00001
Phosphorus	.07	Cerium	.0004	Helium	.0000069

The 57 elements of which there is a measurable amount in seawater. The overwhelming majority is hydrogen and oxygen (96.5%). The table shows the number of parts of the element per million parts of seawater.

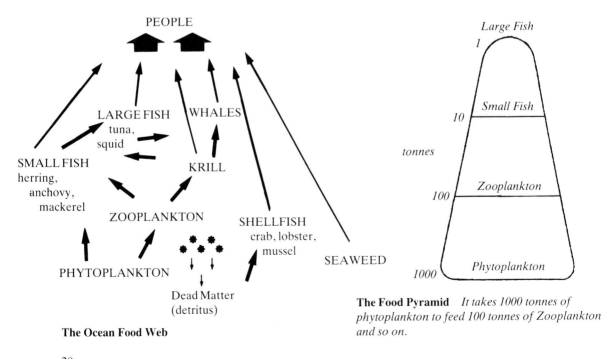

The Ocean Food Web

The Food Pyramid   *It takes 1000 tonnes of phytoplankton to feed 100 tonnes of Zooplankton and so on.*

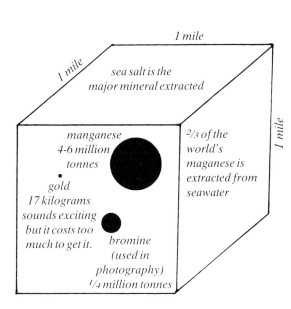

sea salt is the major mineral extracted

1 mile
1 mile
1 mile

manganese
4-6 million
tonnes

gold
17 kilograms
sounds exciting
but it costs too
much to get it.

²/₃ of the world's maganese is extracted from seawater

bromine
(used in photography)
¹/₄ million tonnes

The amount of 3 important elements in a cubic mile of seawater.

What strange creatures live in the ocean deep. Some fish, like these shown here, are translucent – you can see through them!

Mermaids are well known in the mythology of the sea. Half woman, half fish it is probable that they have been "seen" by sailors who were actually looking at seals or manatees – especially if the sailor had had his tot of rum!

The Coelacanth was thought to be extinct until it was rediscovered in 1952 off the coast of Madagascar. A TV film has been made of its life which shows that there are many specimens, but they live deep down in the sea and are rarely caught by fishermen. If they are they can be sold for many hundreds of pounds. The Coelacanth grows to around 1¹/₂ metres (5 feet) in length.

29

Dolphins

The story goes that two boys were windsurfing off the eastern coast of Australia during their summer of 1988. One spotted a shark approaching, so he made rapidly for the shore. His companion was not so fortunate and before he could make his getaway the shark made a lunge at him, luckily biting into the surf board and only grazing his leg. At that moment his friend, who had reached the beach, saw an incredible event. A school of about a dozen dolphins sped towards the victim, swimming at and around the attacking shark. After much flurry and splash the shark was driven off and the dolphins, as if a job had been well done, made off out to sea. The young man reached the safety of the shore and will always believe that he was rescued from death by the dolphins. Whether or not the animals were aware that

Dolphinarium. *The intelligence and skill of dolphins is used to entertain people. Though the display is very enjoyable to most audiences, the question is "Should such beautiful creatures be kept captive just to show us a few tricks?".*

they saved a human being no one can say, perhaps they were only reacting in an instinctive way to a creature which given the chance would have attacked them as well. What we do know is that dolphins are able to communicate with each other and that they have the ability to relate closely to people and to learn tricks. Have you ever seen dolphins performing in an aquarium?

Unfortunately, dolphins feed on fish which humans hunt – in particular anchovies, mackerel and herring. They also swim with tuna and so become entangled in the tuna-fishing nets. They are hunted for their meat and blubber, especially in the Black Sea off Turkey, and off the coast of Japan – where they are often killed in order not to prey on the fish wanted by the Japanese fishermen. Estimates that between 40 and 50 thousand dolphins have been killed accidentally each year in the tuna fisheries of the Pacific Ocean by United States fishing boats have led to laws making it illegal to fish for tuna without using nets through which dolphins can escape. Some boats even have

Decorations on the walls of the ancient Temple of Knossus on the island of Crete show that the dolphin has long been a symbol of beauty and grace. Sailors welcome dolphin packs beside their ship as a sign of good fortune. A dolphin leaping alongside the sea nymph Calypso has been used by the Cousteau Society as their logo.

divers whose job it is to help the dolphins escape. Further north, off the coast of Canada, porpoises – close relatives of the dolphins – are caught by the thousand in the gill nets of the salmon fishers. Another relative of the dolphin is the narwhal. Narwhal tusks are much sought after by dealers – a single tusk can be worth as much as £3000. It is no wonder that, despite a ban on their capture, narwhal hunting still goes on. As with all of the whale family they are vulnerable to hunters when they come to the surface for air.

Jaques Cousteau is famous as an underwater explorer. He saw in dolphins grace, intelligence and beauty: he appreciated the way in which they hunted for food together and protected their families. It seemed to him that the way in which people abused the dolphin was an example of the way people abused the world's environment generally. Like dolphins the ordinary people of the world should work together and in so doing protect and conserve the world. He said:

"We can take our inspiration from the dolphins, who defend themselves and their offspring through an instinct to mass together in the face of danger and to attack power with wisdom".

Jaques Cousteau took the dolphin as the symbol of the Cousteau Society, which he founded to protect the environment of the world's seas and oceans.

Narwhal tusk. *Male narwhals have a tusk up to three metres long. It is a tooth protruding from the mouth. The main use is to stir up the seabed to flush out the flat fish on which it feeds. At mating time it is used as a "duelling" sword against other males.*

31

Jellyfish – Floating Free

It is not only plankton which drift around the seas, moved by the currents and the wind. Some jellyfish drift as the water takes them. Most jellies move themselves by the pump action of their bell or umbrella-shaped bodies, which forces the water out with a jet propulsion action. The drifters, instead, have "sails" which catch the wind and, together with the ocean current, moves them on. Their names – Portuguese Man-of-War for one species and Jack Sail-by-the-Wind for another – emphasize the sailing method of movement. Both of these have hanging tentacles which poison their zooplankton prey.

The Man-of-War is not one animal. It consists of a community of many individual polyps. For each individual the marine biologist gives the name "person". Each fully grown Man-of-War may contain up to a thousand persons. There are four person types, beginning with the remarkable FLOAT PERSON. This is a gas-filled ballon, about 300 mm (one foot) long in adults. The Float Person sticks out of the water by about 150 mm (six inches). The ridge crest, usually coloured blue or pink, lies along the top of the balloon and acts as the sail. The rest of the colony of persons hangs below it.

The second kind of person is the TENTACLE PERSON. These can measure from three to 30 metres in length (10 to 100 feet). A fully grown colony has about eight long tentacles and many of a smaller length. The tentacles are covered with barbed stings called NEMATOCYSTS which are explained in the diagram. When extended, the tentacles can move about searching for food. Anything which touches a tentacle causes a sting to strike, hook itself to the prey and inject poison to stun it. The tentacle then coils itself up, taking the captured meal to the third kind of polyp, the STOMACH PERSON, or GASTEROZOOID, to give it its scientific name. Each of these has a mouth only which both takes in the food for the stomach to digest and ejects the waste matter. The food is digested and transferred to all other parts of the community. Larger fish will be consumed by several stomach persons.

Finally there are the SEX PERSONS known as GONOZOOIDS, which hang as pink clusters

Lateen sail on a Kenyan boat.
Sailors in the fifteenth century thought a Portuguese Man-of-War looked like a Portuguese ship known as a caravel. Its lateen sail was similar to the crest on the jellyfish.

amongst the tentacles. It is known that a Portuguese Man-of-War has either male or female gonozooids, but how reproduction takes place is not known. Infant Men-of-War are found with a small float person and one tentacle, presumably having developed from an egg. It takes about a month for the float to grow to 25 mm (an inch) long, by which time it has grown several tentacles and stomach persons. Four or five months later it has reached adult size. One of the odd features of this jellyfish is that the tentacles develop on one side of the body or the other. Thus some of them have most of their weight on the left hand side making the float tilt to the left, whilst the others have the weight to the right so causing a right-hand side tilt. The result of this is that the wind tends to blow one sort towards the left and the others towards the right. The same wind direction enables the jellyfish to spread out far more than if they all tilted the same way.

Portuguese Men-of-War live mainly in tropical waters but sometimes they are blown on to more northern shores. Although it would take a great many stings to cause a human to die (mainly from the shock, not the poison), jellyfish stings are very painful. The pain usually lasts for only a few hours, although more severe stinging can leave marks for many weeks. Men-of-War are to be avoided, although they provide food for loggerhead and hawksbill turtles and for sunfish. Crabs will feed on stranded jellyfish. One type of octopus is said to break off a tentacle from a Man-of-War and to use it as a poison whip to stun its own prey. In fact, the biggest threat to these floating jellyfish is oil pollution, not other animals.

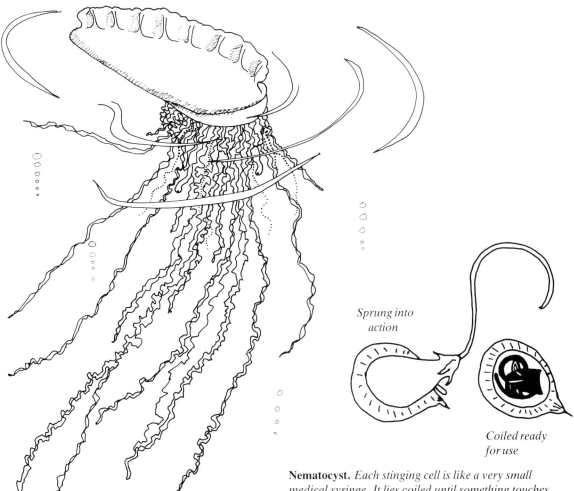

Sprung into action

Coiled ready for use

Portuguese Man-of-War.
Tentacles trail beneath the gas-filled float.

Nematocyst. *Each stinging cell is like a very small medical syringe. It lies coiled until something touches the trigger. The sting springs out, barbs itself on to the prey, pierces the victim and shoots poison down the thread.*

The Ocean Dustbin

There seems to be a common misunderstanding that the oceans of the world provide limitless space in which to dump waste and that salt water will destroy all of the undesirable poisons and bacteria. This is not so, despite the fact that they occupy nearly three quarters of the globe, covering 140 million square miles with depths in places down to seven miles.

Most of the life of the seas is concentrated along the relatively shallow, sunlight-affected, inshore areas of the oceans, accounting for perhaps a tenth of the surface area. As we shall see, it is along the ocean rim that the majority of the people of the world live – and produce the majority of the waste which is poured into it.

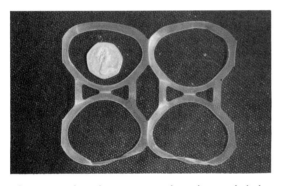

Plastic rings keep beer cans together – but are lethal around the necks of sea birds.

Much of the "waste" which enters the sea is sediment brought down from the erosion of the land by natural processes (estimated to be 9000 million tonnes a year before human interference but now totalling 24,000 million tonnes). Of the material which is artificially dumped into the sea, 80 percent is sediment dredged from river and harbour bottoms. This consists of sand, clay and silt, together with the sewage and other wastes of times past which had settled on the river bed or had been tipped in to the estuary. The dredged sediment is taken to offshore locations and dumped, possibly to be brought back inshore by the sea currents.

The one fifth of waste which is not dredged sediment consists of refuse, sewage and industrial material. This latter includes nuclear waste, chemicals, metals and oil. The majority has been sent on its journey to the ocean by

Shores are littered with plastic waste, fishing nets and other rubbish. Birds, fish, seals and porpoises are often entangled in this flotsam to die in agony.

being deliberately discharged into rivers; some has been taken out to sea to be dumped whilst the rest, particularly the oil, has been deposited as the result of accident. One particular concern is the amount of farm fertilizers which are washed through the soil and on into the rivers.

It is estimated that over 70,000 chemical compounds are made in the world at the present time. Most of them eventually reach the sea – and scientists have no idea what the effect of most of them will be on the ocean. The following chapters will go into each of these particular wastes in greater detail, although they will not tell the whole story. For example, obsolete weapons of war are generally dumped into the oceans. Forty-five years after the end of the Second World War some of the drums of chemical warfare gas dumped in the North Sea have been washed up on shore to reveal the fact that they are leaking their contents.

Metals escape into the sea after industrial processes. Mercury is particularly dangerous, as proved by the now infamous case of Minamata

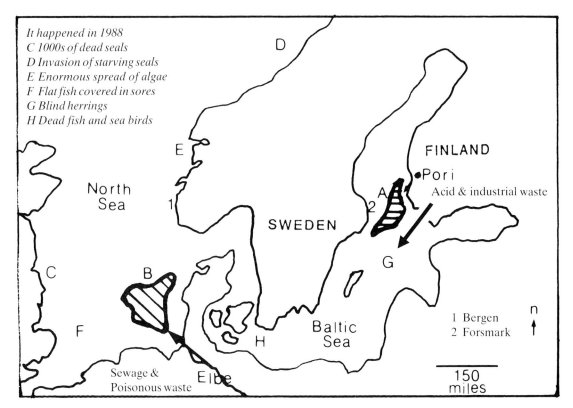

It happened in 1988
C 1000s of dead seals
D Invasion of starving seals
E Enormous spread of algae
F Flat fish covered in sores
G Blind herrings
H Dead fish and sea birds

FINLAND
•Pori
Acid & industrial waste

North Sea

SWEDEN

Baltic Sea

1 Bergen
2 Forsmark

150 miles

Sewage & Poisonous waste

Elbe

The North Sea and Baltic now show every sign of being poisoned with the dumping of waste. A chemical factory at Pori is accused of pouring 80,000 tonnes of sulphuric acid and 50,000 tonnes of iron sulphate into the sea, poisoning an extensive area (A). Sewage and poisonous waste has created an area of deoxygenated water – a 'dead sea' (B).

Bay in Japan. Between 1953 and 1960 mercury discharged into the bay was taken into the bodies of fish, which were caught and eaten by the local people. It affected the brains of unborn babies, even though it seemed to leave the mothers unharmed. People began to twitch, their arms and legs became twisted, some became blind, others went mad or died in terrible pain. The first signs of what was going on were to be seen in the pet cats of the area, which developed symptoms which led to them being called "the dancing cats of Minamata". Unfortunately, it was many years before the connection was made between the industrial waste going into the sea and the disease caused on land. But do we ever learn? At the present time, a similar situation may be developing at the Amazon estuary, where it meets the South Atlantic. Upstream gold prospectors are extracting gold from the river sediment by using mercury, the waste from which is pouring into the sea, presumably to be absorbed by fish along the way.

The quality of the air we breathe is of prime importance to our existence . . . so too is the quality of the water in our oceans.

The North Sea – is it turning into a Dead Sea?

Marine experts have concluded that unless we take urgent action to clean up the North Sea it will be dead by the mid 1990s. From the UK the rivers Thames, Humber, Tees, Tyne and Forth act as conduits for a toxic current of filth. Untreated sewage (five million tonnes annually), cadmium, mercury, oil, chemicals, pesticides and fertilizers pour forth. From continental Europe the Rhine, Elbe and Seine add enormous quantities of poisonous waste and fertilizer-rich water to the North Sea. Cyanide, lead, phosphate and dioxin are slowly killing every form of water life. In 1987 over 500 oil spillages were recorded. Disasters like the destruction of the Piper Alpha oil platform add to the pollution. Garbage from the ships in one of the busiest sea routes in the world provides extra rubbish. As the North sea is almost "self contained" there is little natural flushing out of its water, with the narrow English Channel at one end and the Norwegian Sea at the other.

Oil Pollution

On 6 July 1988 a disastrous fire on the North Sea oil rig *Piper Alpha* caused the deaths of 167 workmen. It did not cause the oil pollution which was at first expected, probably because the intense fire burned the oil as it poured out of the undersea well. With the accident to the oil rig *Ixtoc 1* it was different. For 295 days, until March 1980, oil had escaped into the open ocean of the Gulf of Mexico. Altogether 140 million gallons, well over three million barrels, had poured into the sea – of which only about six million gallons were recovered: 134 million gallons remained to pollute the water and the nearby shores. Other accidents involving oil rigs at sea or the pipelines which fill the giant oil tankers have been the cause of oil spreads on the sea: these large patches are known as "oil slicks".

Most oil refineries are located beside the sea or alongside river estuaries only a few miles from the open sea. Accidents and oil seepage occur frequently, so much so that it has been estimated that 200,000 tonnes of oil pollute the oceans from this source every year. Oil floats on the surface of the water so that one tonne which

Offshore oil platform.
A typical oil well platform at sea. (Off Benin, a West African country bordering with Nigeria.)

An accidental oil spillage near Hastings.
Lumps of oil float on the water and collect in sticky masses on the beach.

Tar ball. Thick oil forms a ball as it is washed up and down on the shore. Known as tar balls, they are really oil sludge dumped by ships.

spreads out to a thickness of 10cm can cover an area about the size of a football pitch.

Where television, radio news and newspapers are concerned it is the occasional accident to oil tankers which claims most attention. The most famous of these was the shipwreck of the *Torrey Canyon* off the coast of South-West England in 1967. Little was known of the way to deal with such a hazard at that time and the spread of the oil leak was viewed with horror. In the end the government sent in bomber planes to sink the ship completely, but even then, as with other sunken vessels, oil continued to seep to the surface from its tanks. Nevertheless, pollution from accidents is only a minor matter in comparison with other sources of oil pollution. The deliberate outwash of waste oil from the tanks of ships is a far more usual source of harm. International agreements have led to a great reduction in this sort of pollution but, as the pictures show, it still happens.

Other major sources of oil pollution are from natural seepages from oil bearing rocks on the seabed and from the spillages from factories near to rivers or the sea shores.

Various types of detergent chemicals have been developed to disperse oil slicks and in most parts of the world there are anti-oil-pollution boats waiting to tackle oil spills as they occur, in a similar way to the engines waiting at a fire station to deal with any fires which break out.

The Mediterranean sea is often affected by oil spillage. Unfortunately for its beaches, many of the large oil production countries are around its shores. Oil pollution from the tanker docks and from the refineries of Libya and Tunisia in North Africa is a particular menace. It is very difficult to trace the source of any escaped oil unless the leak itself is seen.

Oiled sea birds.
An RSPCA officer displays a few of the seabirds killed by the oil spill. Many hundreds more float out to sea never to be found.

Corexit (Corrects it!)

A new oil dispersant called Corexit is now in use. It works by altering the surface tension of oil and water so that the oil sinks below the surface. It needs fairly rough seas to cause the oil and water to mix. What happens to marine life below the surface? Out of sight out of mind!

Oil skimmers

Oil skimmers are like water vacuum cleaners. They skim the surface of the water, drawing in the top layer which contains the spilt oil. The oil is retained in the machine while the clean water is returned to the sea.

Oil Disaster – The *Exxon Valdez*

The Place: Prince William Sound, Alaska, USA
The Day: Good Friday, 24 March 1989
The Time: Just after midnight
The Ship: The oil tanker *Exxon Valdez*,
        300 metres long, 95,000 tonnes
Speed: Eight knots
The Captain: Joseph Hazelwood
The duty helmsman: Third mate Greg Cousins
The accident: The tanker was heading for the open sea from the oil terminal of Valdez, laden with crude oil from the Alaskan oil field. The tanker hit a reef, damaging its starboard oil tanks. Two miles further on it ran aground on another reef. The tanker was even more seriously holed.
The Result: At least ELEVEN MILLION GALLONS of crude oil flowed out into the sea. Within a short time five square miles of sea were affected. Two days later it was 100 square miles and continued to spread.
The Treatment: The first dispersants were applied after 6.45pm on Easter Sunday – nearly two days later!

Such are the "scenario" details of what is expected to become the worst ship oil pollution disaster for the USA and probably the world. Like all accidents, it should never have happened. Only the enquiry into the incident will reveal why the ship was off course in uncharted waters, why the captain was not on the bridge and why it took so long for any remedial treatment to be applied. The captain has been charged with negligence.

Look at the map of the ocean currents (page 5) and you will see that the Alaskan current may well carry the crude oil into the North Pacific Ocean, were it will be spread by the other ocean movements. Nevertheless it is the effect on the Alaskan area, one of the few areas in the world of untouched nature, that is the major concern. The seas are the home and breeding places for sea otters, whales, salmon, herring and a variety of other fish. The accident happened at the time of the annual salmon run through the Prince

Off loading the *Exxon Valdez*.
The smaller Exxon Baton Rouge *tanker offloads the remaining oil from the wrecked* Exxon Valdez. *They are surrounded by oil covered water which is prevented from spreading by the boom stretching from top left to middle right. The small boat to starboard (the right) of the* Valdez *leaves an oil free trail as it cuts through the spillage.*

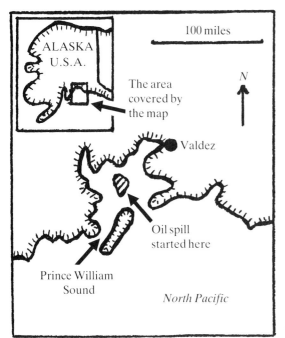

Prince William Sound, Alaska.

Aircraft spread detergent on the Valdez *oil spillage.*

Prince William Sound, Alaska.

The inset map shows Alaska, USA and the location of Prince William Sound. The Alaskan pipeline ends at Valdez where the stricken ship loaded its cargo of crude oil. The accident happened soon after it left port.

William Sound on their way to their spawning grounds in the Gulkana, Tazlina and other rivers around Valdez. The herring shoals were heading out to sea to provide one of the main catches for the local fishermen. Sea birds abound in these food rich seas and on land brown bears and other animals prey on the salmon which move inland. Millions – quite literally millions – of birds, fish and mammals have been killed. It is impossible to count their numbers. Perhaps the most pathetic for the animal rescue teams is to find the many oil smothered bodies of young sea otters "drowned" in a thick layer of crude oil.

The crude oil reaches Valdez by pipe line from the north of Alaska. Its creation and its operation have been heavily criticized by environmentalists. But prosperity has been brought to the region, where the local people not only pay little tax but receive direct payment as some reward for the disturbance brought by the oil industry. Plans are in hand to extract oil from the rest of Alaska. The *Exxon Valdez* disaster reminds people of the real price that may have to be paid. Difficult conservation decisions have to be made.

Who pays and how much?

In a road accident, the blame and the damage done can be assessed. If oil is spilled it may not be possible to attribute the blame precisely or to quantify the damage caused. For instance, what is the value in money of a dead sea bird?

In 1969 an oil pollution incident off California killed many sea birds. It was decided in court that birds and other animals did have a value. At first it was put at an inadequate $1 but by 1976 the value of a seagull was put at $10 and a swan at $200.

What about the money lost when tourists stay away from resorts with polluted beaches? How can this be calculated and who might receive compensation?

Who do you think should have paid for the *Torrey Canyon* disaster when I tell you that
  the crew was Italian
    the ship was registered in Liberia
      it was insured in London
        owned by Union Oil of California
          subleased to Barracuda Tankers Ltd
            who subleased it to BP
              but was being used by Petroleum Trading Ltd?
Eventually the British and French governments seized and sold a sister ship as recompense and obtained $7½ million from the insurers – but you cannot measure conservation issues with cash values.

Dumping Sewage in the Sea

The natural processes of living creatures which take in food and expel waste provide important soil nutrients needed by plants. Included also are bacteria, some of which are harmful to people. Human waste – sewage – is offensive to us by sight and smell. Nevertheless, farmyard manure is spread on fields as a fertilizer and, in some countries like China and India, sewage is used in a similar way. In our own country sewage treated at a purification works can become an odourless, safe and valuable fertilizer. The treated or part treated sewage is known as sewage sludge.

The full treatment of sewage is very expensive compared with simply dumping the raw sewage or sludge in the sea or in a river leading to the sea. The natural reaction of the salt water with it will result in the waste becoming harmless unless there is far too much for the sea water to alter, or there is insufficient time for the reaction to be completed before it is washed back on to the shore. In early 1989 a

Sewage Outfall. Outfalls may be clearly marked, or they may be recognized by shrewd observation.

report confirmed that a third of the beaches in the UK were so badly contaminated with sewage that they were well below the minimum standard of cleanliness acceptable to the European Economic Community.

A usual answer to the problem of beach contamination is to build longer discharge pipes, which will carry the sewage further away from the shore. Wherever there are people there will be a sewage disposal problem. In the UK there are proper lavatories and an underground sewer pipe system to carry the effluent away. It is not the same everywhere. For instance on the coast of Africa, beside the Atlantic Ocean, eight million people live in Lagos, the capital of Nigeria. Many of them do have primitive sanitary arrangements but others have none and need to use the beaches and lagoons as toilets. It has been estimated that seven-and-a-half million litres of raw sewage were put into the Iddo lagoon during one three month period in 1974.

Around the coasts of the world the problems of sewage disposal are widespread. Japan and China on one side of the North Pacific Ocean,

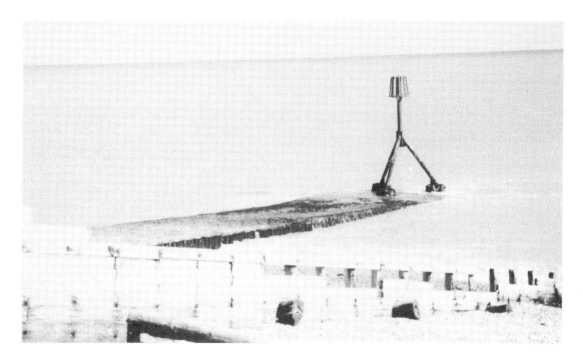

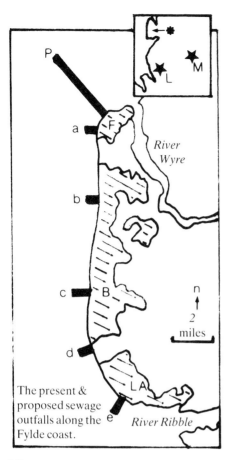

The present &
proposed sewage
outfalls along the
Fylde coast.

Outfalls

P Proposed	**L** Liverpool
a Chatsworth	**M** Manchester
b Anchorsholme	**F** Fleetwood
c Manchester Square	**B** Blackpool
d Airport	**LA** Lytham St Annes
e Fairhaven	

The Fylde coast is shown by the asterisk on the inset map.

Sewage disposal along the Fylde Coast.

The Fylde coast is the holiday area of north-west England. Blackpool is world famous for its beaches and tower. Yet those beaches and the others along the 20 miles of seashore are the most polluted in Britain. Four short pipes stretch out to sea and pour 68 million litres of untreated sewage into the water EVERY DAY. It is proposed to replace three of the pipes with one outfall sewer three miles long. Opponents of the scheme claim that this will not cure the problem of beach contamination unless the sewage is first cleaned in an inland works.

Anyhow if it clears the Blackpool beaches what about Morecambe Bay to the north – will the sewage collect there?

Mexico, the USA and Canada on the other, send sewage into the sea as do the countries with seashores in South America. With over 950 million people living along the shores of India, Pakistan, Bangladesh, Sri Lanka and the Maldive Islands, coastal pollution from sewage is very serious. Almost as bad are the waters along the shores of Eastern Asia where the Philippines, Malaysia and Thailand are badly affected. Yet neighbouring Singapore has tackled the problem so well that 97 per cent of its population now uses modern sanitation with sewage treatment. The sea around Singapore has shown a five times decrease in sewage contamination between 1980 and 1985.

Soiled bathing beaches are very unpleasant, unsightly and unhygienic. Sewage (and chemical) pollution affects the quality of the fish and shellfish caught for food. Partially enclosed seas like the Caribbean and enclosed seas like the Mediterranean are particularly vulnerable to contamination. The Mediterranean coast is one of the most popular in the world for holidays, yet it was one of the worst affected from sewage pollution. In 1985 the 18 Mediterranean countries adopted common minimum standards for water cleanliness. Combined action by their governments in providing better sewage treatment has meant that the sea water and the holiday beaches are now much cleaner than in the past. Yet in 1989 the beaches of Rimini and other seaside resorts of the Northern Adriatic (that part of the Mediterranean between Italy and Yugoslavia) were covered with a brown algal slime, the result of sewage pollution spread from the River Po.

Better sewage disposal costs a lot of money but we must ask again can we count the cost of improvement of the environment in cash only?

Bathing Forbidden. *In any language the effect of the fouling of beaches by sewage is quite clear.*

Carry on Dumping

Unfortunately, the problem of sewage disposal is complicated by the fact that effluent, from urban areas in particular, contains industrial waste. Although there are strict controls on the toxicity (poison content) of factory discharge, much of it contains metals dangerous to plants and creatures and even more poisonous chemicals. Some poisons get into the sewage system after they have been used on farms to kill weeds and insects.

The ideal way to dispose of sewage is yet to be found. Of the 30 million tonnes produced each year in the UK four per cent is burnt, 27 per cent is buried in old quarries, 39 per cent is spread on the land and 30 per cent is dumped at sea. All methods have their disadvantages.

It is sea disposal which is of interest to us in this book. Certainly all raw sewage needs to be treated before disposal at sea. In some parts of the world the practice is to load sewage sludge on to barges and to take it out to sea to be dumped as with London and, until recently,

Dumping London's sewage.
Up to 12,000 tonnes of treated sewage sludge are dumped daily from four specially made boats into the Thames estuary.
A Barrow Deep Dump site
B Black Deep (dump site now disused)
C Gravesend
D The Mud Reaches near Beckton

with New York. London's sludge is dumped in the Barrow Deep off the mouth of the River Thames. It is one thing to dump sludge, to keep it there is another. Tides and currents will return sewage back to the shore from the ends of pipes or from the dump sites. Investigation has shown that sewage sludge has returned up the Thames with strong traces being found near Gravesend and Rainham, the latter only a few miles from the centre of the capital city.

Deep ocean sludge disposal has been proposed. It would be discharged from huge tanker ships into the abyssal depths at least 4000 metres (nearly three miles) below the surface. A close inspection of the deep seabed will be necessary first of all to determine that too much damage will not be done to marine life.

The cause of most concern is the loss of oxygen in the water as a result of the presence of sewage and also the nitrates which run off into rivers from farmland. Nutritious sewage sludge material will feed plant life within the oceans. In particular, simple plants known as algæ will "bloom". They will grow in abundance, die and rot away to use up much of the oxygen in the process. The water becomes "deoxygenated" and useless to most living things. This is called HYPERTROPHICATION. The organic matter (it was once alive) in the sewage sludge will also rot and use up oxygen. Fish and other creatures cannot live in deoxygenated water, so

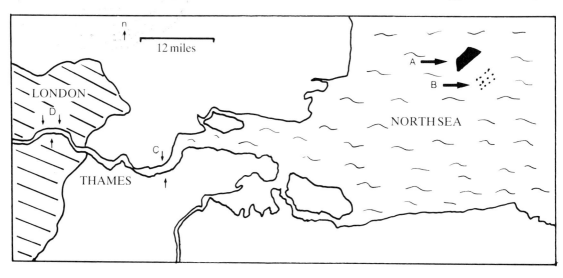

that, to all intents and purposes, the sea is "dead". Many river estuaries become deoxygenated too, for instance Chesapeake Bay to the south of New York. Once famous for its seafood, the bay no longer produces oysters, crabs or other shellfish.

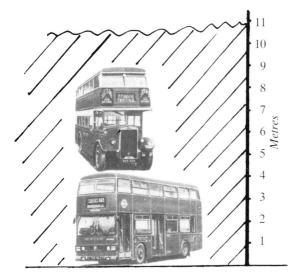

New York sewage.
In 1981 sea disposal of sewage sludge from New York was banned – but not until it had reached over 11 metres (35 feet) in depth over wide areas of the seabed off the coast of the city. Enough and more to cover two double decker buses!

Beach polluted

Porthmeor Beach at St Ives, Cornwall, which holds EEC awards for cleanliness, has been polluted with raw sewage on successive days this week. South-West Water said it drifted ashore from a sea outfall because of unusual weather conditions.

Algae clean-up

The Italian parliament has approved a £600 million fund to clean up the Adriatic, where rotting algae washed up on holiday beaches has badly affected tourism. The three-year programme will improve sewage systems and reduce effluent from the Po and other rivers. — Reuter

One week in August 1989.
Sewage pollution problems reported from Italy and England. The common excuse when things go wrong with sea disposal of sewage is "unusual weather conditions"!

Proposed deep sea disposal of sewage sludge.

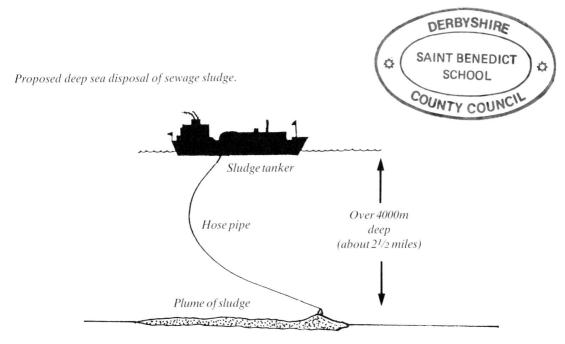

Marine Incineration of Waste

One of the most controversial methods which deals with toxic (poisonous) waste has been to incinerate (burn) it at sea, well away from the land. Specially constructed incineration ships can destroy 99.9 per cent of the dangerous chemicals with which they are loaded.

The company which operates a fleet of ships

Marine Incineration.
Even PCBs will change into water and hydrochloric acid at 1350°C. The water is harmless and the acid will disperse in the vastness of the sea. Despite this theory, the dense clouds of smoke show that plenty of pollutants are discharged to add to air pollution and contribute to acid rain and the Greenhouse Effect.

(the Vulcanus Fleet) in the North Sea maintains that no damage is done to the sea, except beneath the plume of exhaust itself. The method appears to offer a cheap, easy and safe way to dispose of some highly toxic wastes which may well cause a serious risk to health if disposed of on land. One leading scientist, Professor R.B. Clark, the editor of the Marine Pollution Bulletin, describes the hazards associated with waste burnt at sea as "miniscule" . . . . BUT others disagree, notably the members of the Greenpeace organization. They have prevented incineration on several occasions.

Even if it is accepted that modern incineration destroys all but 0.1 per cent of the waste – which sounds fine – this means that for every tonne of material burnt, one kilogramme of waste remains. With an estimated 100 million tonnes being involved, the significant amount of 100,000 tonnes remains unburnt. Environmentalists believe that even more stays unburnt and the plume of exhaust reaches up into the upper air. As with smoke from a factory, it is carried by the wind to pollute other countries.

Most important of all, the idea that whatever falls into the sea will be diluted so much that it will be harmless is being challenged. A thin oily film, called the LIPID MICROLAYER, is present on the surface of the sea. It is only as thick as a one penny piece at its maximum, but it is in this very top layer of the ocean that many larvae of fish and other sea creatures, such as plankton, live. The Petrel and several other sea birds skim off this water layer to collect these morsels of food. Unfortunately, it is in this layer that the leftover toxic pollutants accumulate and these may include the most deadly of poisons, the non-biodegradable (it will not rot away) DIOXIN. They are of obvious harm to the larvae and the plankton and to the birds which feed on them.

At the second North Sea Conference of European States in November 1987, it was agreed that marine incineration in the North Sea should cease by 1994. At a later international conference, known as the London Dumping Convention, it was agreed to stop marine incineration of noxious liquid wastes worldwide by the same year 1994. This decision does not include the incineration of rubbish or of oil waste, both of which cause gases to rise into the atmosphere.

Perhaps the greatest benefit from halting incineration at sea will be that alternative methods of disposal, or of preventing the production of the waste in the first place, will now be forced upon industry. The cheap marine incineration method will no longer exist.

At the second North Sea conference it was also decided to:

i. ban the discharge of plastics and other synthetic material into the North Sea

ii. allow other refuse (glass, metal, paper, china and edible waste) to be thrown into the North Sea

Nuclear Waste

There is no need for me to tell you that radioactive nuclear waste is very dangerous to people's health. Most especially it can lead to cancer, which includes leukaemia, cancer of the blood. Nuclear material can be used for weapons of war and we all know how dreadful atomic war could be. Fortunately, radioactive material can be used to benefit rather than destroy humankind. Electrical production, medical treatment and industrial processes use nuclear reactions to our advantage, but unwelcome waste is produced. This is divided into three categories:

Low level waste This includes liquid, clothing and other materials which have been in contact with radioactivity.

Intermediate level waste This is all the solids and liquids from nuclear power stations and industrial plants.

High level waste This is concentrated highly active nuclear material which though it is "spent" continues to give out a great deal of radiation.

Most of the disposal methods for this waste are carried out on land. The sea is used but generally on a decreased scale. Low level liquid waste can be pumped out to sea along pipelines, as at Sellafield in the North of England.

Low level and intermediate level waste packed in steel drums encased in concrete was dumped in the sea by Britain until 1982. This took place in an internationally agreed area of the Atlantic Ocean some 800 kilometres from Lands End. In response to an international

Sea access/seabed disposal.
Similar techniques to oil-well drilling may be used to prepare shafts deep beneath the ocean bed.

agreement on sea disposal this method was stopped. In 1988 the British Government announced that it would not renew the disposal of drummed nuclear waste at sea but, at a later date, it might decide to sink large items of radioactive waste taken from disused nuclear power stations.

The USA dumped about 90,000 barrels of low level waste at sea between 1946 and 1970, when the operation was suspended. Investigations in the San Francisco locality showed that many of the dumped barrels were corroded and leaking.

Inshore disposal.

A pipeline under the sea discharges waste into the Irish Sea from Sellafield. It is claimed to be free of nuclear contamination but Greenpeace members challenge this, and have spent much time blocking the outlet. This has led to court proceedings.

Sellafield

Irish Sea

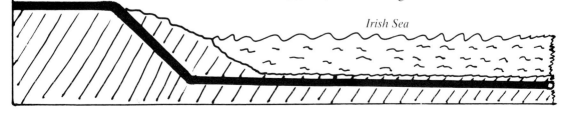

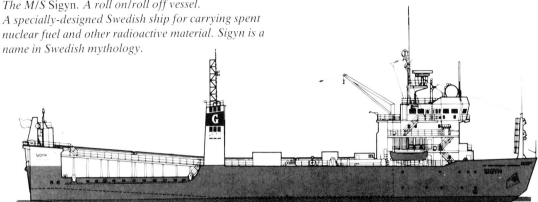

The M/S Sigyn. A roll on/roll off vessel.
A specially-designed Swedish ship for carrying spent
nuclear fuel and other radioactive material. Sigyn is a
name in Swedish mythology.

Opponents of dumping at sea have always claimed that salt water was one of the most corrosive of liquids and that eventually even the most protected of nuclear waste would leak from the cannisters. Despite these fears, plans are still in hand to dump nuclear waste, even waste with a high level of radioactivity. The idea is to "vitrify" it, which means to solidify it in glass. This will be kept in a safe store for 50 or more years until it has "cooled" and lost much of its activity. This waste may then be placed in the very deepest parts of the ocean, packed into holes drilled in the sea bed.

Less dramatic than this are plans to bury low level and intermediate level waste in a "repository", which will consist of a series of tunnels and vaults constructed under the sea bed and reached either from the shore or from floating platforms out to sea.

Under seabed disposal sites are being considered by the UK Nirex Ltd, the company responsible for the disposal of low and intermediate level waste. Other countries, such as Japan, are still investigating deep-sea disposal and plan better methods to prevent sea-water corrosion of the containers. As with sewage, the ocean movements will spread any nuclear contamination around the world.

Swedish nuclear waste disposal.
At Forsmark, Sweden, (see map on page 35) the first loads of nuclear waste were put under the Baltic Sea in 1988. The site is a kilometre from the shore. It has two main access tunnels, four disposal caverns and one deeper silo.

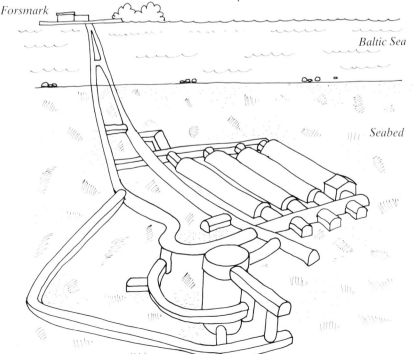

Forsmark

Baltic Sea

Seabed

Power from the Seas

The water in the sea moves from one place to another and up-and-down as the surface currents drift around the oceans and the waves and tides rise and fall. The water in the sea is at a different temperature both from one area and another, and between the surface and ocean depths. These movements and temperature differences are a potential source of electric power – an alternative to nuclear energy or burning fossil fuels. There have been many ideas for using the sea as a power source, either directly to harness the force of the water itself or converting it into electricity.

Tide mills are quite common, though few are still operational. At Woodbridge, in Suffolk, one was built over 800 years ago and was at work until quite recently. Thirty-two tide mill sites are known to have existed in Devon and Cornwall. How does a tide mill work? The rising tide is trapped in a reservoir and, as it falls, the water is allowed to escape via a water wheel which turns the machinery. The 13-hour tidal cycle meant work times varied daily, which was unpopular with millers and customers.

Electricity production
The idea of "free" electricity from a limitless non-polluting energy source is very attractive, but the technological problems are very difficult and usually the machinery is very expensive to manufacture. So far there are only a few ocean-powered electricity schemes in operation commercially, providing power for homes and businesses. Around the world there are many experimental schemes, some of which may prove to be worth further development. One problem is how to connect the electricity production system to the distribution grid, particularly where the power source is out at sea. This is an expensive difficulty to overcome.

Of the schemes producing electricity the best known are in:

France: The Rance Tidal Power Station
Situated across the mouth of the River Rance near St Malo, a power plant is capable of making 240 megawatts of electricity from its 24 10 megawatt turbines. Unlike the turbines of hydro-electric schemes, which only need to deal with a water flow in one direction, the tidal turbines have to operate with water which flows in both directions as the tide comes in and goes out.

Norway
There are two working experimental power stations using wave power at Toftestallen, near Bergen

Tapchan Power Plant – 1985
Waves flow into a narrow channel to fill a reservoir. The trapped water is then released via electricity-producing turbines. About 350 kilowatts of power can be made. The Norwegians claim that power stations able to produce 300 megawatts can be built using this method.

Oscillating Water Column – 1985
As the waves rise and fall inside a cylinder, air is forced out of the top. This turns an air turbine. As the water falls, air is sucked back in and also turns the turbine. Electricity is made by both

The Ormat Solar Power Plant.
Beit Ha'arava on the Dead Sea uses the high salinity to convert solar energy into electricity. The picture shows the collecting ponds with the power station behind. The method used is described on page 51.

Oscillating Water Column.
The cylindrical installation at Toftestallen has produced power since 1985.

the rise and fall of the water. On average, 500 kilowatts of power production is possible at present.

Hawaii
Ocean Thermal Energy Conversion Plant Hawaii – 1979 (page 51)

The surfaces of the oceans absorb most of the heat from the rays of the sun, which means that the water in the top layer is much warmer than the water deeper down. This is specially true in tropical latitudes. If the warm water is used to evaporate a chemical, usually ammonia, the gas given off can drive a turbine to generate electricity. Cold water from the deep can be pumped to cool the gas back into liquid form once more.

Deep Ocean Water Cooling Hawaiian Power Station

A power station on the Hawaiian coast draws very cold water up from the ocean deep. It cools the used steam back into water. The increased efficiency of the cooling saves nearly $500,000 a year. The deep water is rich in nutrients, which are used for fish-farm activities.

Ideas for Power

Many ideas have been put forward to gather the energy of the oceans and to create electricity. Most are still only experimental. Here are some of them.

Oscillating Vanes ("Ducks")

Each vane is linked to the next through a rotary pump to make a long line of objects which bob up and down as the waves move (they look like bobbing ducks!). The rotary pumps turn an electricity generator. There are many technical problems, which include passing the power to the shore. In order to equal the power produced in a small 2000 megawatt power station, a 250 mile line of ducks would be needed (as far as London is from Newcastle-on-Tyne).

Rafts

Instead of "ducks", large rafts are connected to each other with a hydraulic ram. This consists of a piston in a cylinder which moves back and forth as the waves move the rafts. A fluid is pumped out of the ram through a generator to make power.

Rectifier Locks

As a wave rises, the water is allowed to enter a slot with a flap, in the same way as a letter enters the letter box in your door. As the wave falls, the water now inside the lock compartment falls as well and flows out of another slot at the bottom. As the water falls it is made to turn an electric generator.

A line of ducks.
The movement up and down of the "ducks" generates electricity.

Clams (the original looked a little like the two shells of a clam shellfish)

A clam is made of a concrete cylinder which floats, sealed at both ends with an air bladder attached along its front. As a wave crashes into the clam, air will be forced out of the bladders into the cylinder. As the wave falls, air will be drawn back into the bladder. With an air turbine suspended in the concrete tube, the movement of the air in and out will turn the turbine and create power. In another version, the air bags are in a ring.

Tidal Barrages in the UK

The two most publicized tidal barrage schemes are those across the Mersey and the Severn. If the Severn Barrage was begun now, it is likely that its proposed 7000 megawatts of electricity (about 5 per cent of the UK needs) could be fed into the grid by the year 2000. Original estimates of £4 thousand million have been revised to £8.5 thousand million and are likely in practice to prove even greater. Part of the estuary has now been declared a Site of Special Scientific Interest (SSSI), which will cause planning difficulties.

Open Coast Barrages

Instead of blocking estuaries, it may be possible to build barrages off shore along the open coast, as off Lincolnshire. Barrages would not need to be built very high to cope with tidal ranges of six metres. Forty-five per cent of the tidal energy could be used, compared with 30 per cent for estuaries. Expensive navigation locks would not be necessary and marsh areas for birds would

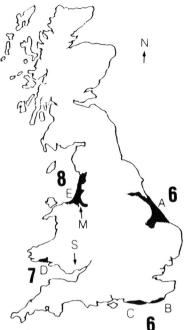

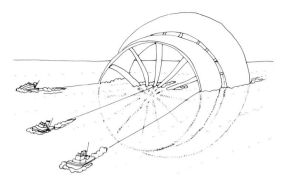

Ocean Current Turbines.
As with all ocean power schemes the equipment could become a hazard to shipping.

Saline Power
Fresh water and salt water come together where rivers meet the sea. If a tank could be built into which flowed fresh water at the bottom and sea water at the top, there would be made a "salinity gradient", that is a difference in saltiness between the top and bottom. With a thin plastic sheet to separate the two waters, through which only fresh water can move, a flow of salt water out of the top will take place. This flow can be "captured" and used to turn an electricity generator. The salinity gradient in salt water inland seas, like the Dead Sea, could also be used to make power.

OTEC. *Many designs for Ocean Thermal Energy Conversion plants exist. The size of the ship gives you some idea of the size of this installation.*

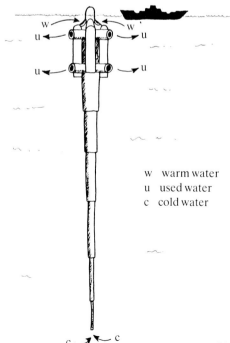

w warm water
u used water
c cold water

Open Coast sites
A Lincolnshire and the Wash
B Hastings Coast
C Brighton Coast
D Carmarthen Bay
E North Wales and Lancashire

Estuary Sites
S Severn estuary
M Mersey estuary

Possible tidal power sites for England and Wales. *The figures indicate the height difference between low and high water in metres with the biggest tides. Open coast barrages need not be built very high. It is claimed 45 per cent of the energy could be used as against 30 per cent with estuary barrages. Mud flats for wading birds would still be available. Navigation locks would be unnecessary. Wind power turbines could be sited on the barrage away from the land where they could be unsightly.*

not be affected. Wind power machines could be sited on the barrage away from land, where they can be unsightly.

Ocean Current Turbine
The surface water of the oceans moves around the world in a fairly fixed pattern. These ocean currents, such as the Gulf Stream Drift, move at fairly steady speeds of three or more knots (the way in which speed is measured at sea). It might be possible to have a series of turbines "hanging" in the moving current and so generate electricity.

The Oceans and the Greenhouse Effect

Warming of the Earth's atmosphere appears to be taking place. Most scientists who study the climate agree on a prediction that the world will be 1.5°C to 4.5°C warmer on average by the year 2030.

If the air warms so too will the sea. The reason for this warming is generally attributed to a climatic phenomenon known as the Greenhouse Effect. A greenhouse used to grow plants will become very warm as the sun shines upon the glass. The diagram shows why the inside heats up. In a similar way, the heat from the sun – short wave radiation – is absorbed by the earth and radiated back into space as long wave heat. Some of it is absorbed by the natural gases present in the air to cause the atmosphere to remain warm. Until recently, most of this escaped into space: this appears no longer to be true.

Over the last 150 years, most of the power for industry has come from burning fossil fuel, mainly coal. The fuel has given off exhaust from chimneys. In the 1950s in the UK the sootiness of the exhaust was cleaned and smokeless zones were introduced – but the gases, mostly invisible, remained. Amongst these gases is carbon dioxide (CO_2). It readily absorbs heat and by so doing, like the greenhouse glass, prevents its escape into the atmosphere. Methane, the gas produced by the decay of sewage, Chlorofluorocarbons (CFCs used in aerosols, refrigerators, air conditioners, and in the manufacture of foam filler and packaging) and other gases also absorb heat. These are called the Greenhouse Gases, because, like the greenhouse, they trap the heat.

It is thought that the world heating will be uneven and that the Arctic and Antarctic areas will be most affected. It is here that much of the water of the world is stored up as ice. It is obvious that the ice caps will melt with that of Antarctica the area most affected. Already large lumps of ice have broken from the ice sheet: one as large as the territory of Hong Kong floated away in 1988. Gradually the Antarctic ice sheet adds more water to the oceans of the world and so causes a rise in sea level. More significant is the expansion of the sea water as the world gradually warms up.

Warm water occupies more space than cold water. It is this expansion which will cause most of the sea level rise.

The complete melting of the ice at the South Pole would cause a 60 metre rise in sea level world wide. This is unlikely to happen, but a rise of over one metre is anticipated. Flooding of low land will be widespread.

Millions of people live in cities beside the ocean edge. London, New York, Calcutta, Tokyo, Melbourne, and Rio de Janeiro are but a few of the world cities that would be flooded if the sea level rose by only a relatively small amount. The fairly new Thames Barrier, erected to protect Central London from floods caused by high tides, will be too low to prevent a similar problem due to a rise in sea level. Low-lying countries like Holland are at risk as well. Sea water is salt, so where it floods the land it poisons the soil for many crops, even when the water itself has gone. People will be forced from these areas as refugees, which could develop into a crisis compared to the Ethiopian famines of recent years.

Carbon dioxide (CO_2) is removed from the air by plants, which means that there is less to

A greenhouse – the way it "works".

Short-wave rays from the sun (1) pass through the greenhouse glass (G) and are absorbed (2) by the floor (F) and other objects. Some rays (3) are reflected back into space. Long wave heat (4) is radiated back into the greenhouse. Most of it is reflected (5) back into the building to heat the air inside. Only a little (6) escapes. The interior of the greenhouse warms up.

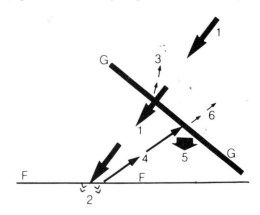

"It'll be up here in about five years!"

The Thames Barrier near Greenwich.

*Cartoonists exaggerate events but often make the point far better than words. Rising sea-level will need to have precautions taken, such as the raising of sea walls, – perhaps not houses on stilts! (*Shropshire Star and Daily Telegraph, *13 April 1989).*

The Thames Barrier near Greenwich.
Semi-circular shields rotate between the towers when it is necessary to block the incoming tide as happened with the Marchioness *pleasure boat tragedy in August 1989.*

warm the atmosphere. Phytoplankton act in a similar way to other vegetation to absorb CO_2, so that the huge plankton blooms mentioned earlier have a most important CO_2 absorbtion action to perform. They are a vital control on global warming. Another book in this series, *The Greenhouse Effect and Ozone Layer*, discusses the whole problem and its possible solutions.

FISHY EVIDENCE!

Unusual tropical fish are reported to be moving into British waters, according to marine biologists. Since 1980, several of these species have been found off the Cornish coast. This seems to indicate a warming of the sea as a result of the Greenhouse Effect.
Source: *The Times*, August 1989.

Down Below in Davy Jones's Locker

An acronym means using the initial letters of a phrase to give a title. For example, the World Health Organization is known as WHO. Sometimes acronyms turn into recognizable and accepted words long after the original meaning of the letters have been forgotten. Scuba diving is a popular way to explore beneath the sea, developed mainly by Jaques Cousteau and his team of divers. Scuba is an acronym of Self-Contained Underwater Breathing Apparatus – but who remembers the way it got its name now? Scuba divers are limited to the upper parts of the ocean and do not venture deep down into the places where early sailors claimed that Davy Jones, the "fiend of the sea", lived, surrounded by the bodies of drowned seamen.

Very high pressures mean that, further down, safer ways have to be found if people are to venture to greater depths. Pressurized diving suits allow this but they are cumbersome and difficult to work in. Bathyspheres are round underwater craft which enable people to descend to great depths. Some are designed to allow the occupants to go outside and swim free, before they return to the sphere. As divers rise to the surface, great care is taken to avoid "the bends", a very dangerous condition where nitrogen bubbles are formed in the blood stream when the pressure on the body drops too quickly.

For really deep-sea exploration, people have to step aside and leave it to machines: echo sounders, gravity recorders, magnetometers, heat sensors, and cameras (both for photography and television). Drilling from vessels at the surface has given us information of the ocean floor but our knowledge is still very limited, just as if we only learnt about the earth's surface from holes drilled miles apart from an airship high above the clouds.

However, there are ways to map the ocean floor which give accurate impressions. GLORIA (an acronym for Geological Long Range Inclined Asdic) is a device which is towed behind a research vessel and which, from just below the surface of the sea, uses long-range side-scan sonar (echo sounding) to build up a picture of the ocean bed. Television combined with robots enables visual exploration to be made with the added ability to pick up samples from the sea bed. One such system is called Argo and Jason. It is named after *Argo*, the craft in which Jason and the Argonauts sailed in search of the Golden Fleece – a story you ought to read if you do not know it already. Look at the illustration to see how it works.

One point of interest is that the fibre optic cables which the system uses to transmit the pictures from the ocean bottom are made of such fine strands of glass that a five mile length

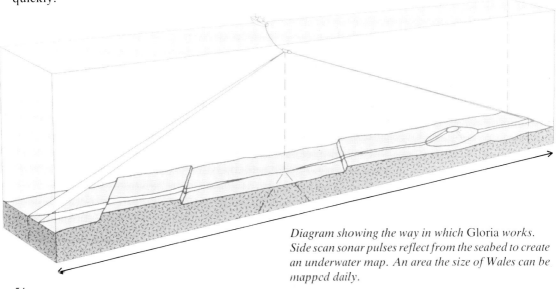

Diagram showing the way in which Gloria *works. Side scan sonar pulses reflect from the seabed to create an underwater map. An area the size of Wales can be mapped daily.*

Underwater map "drawn" by Gloria. Off the coast of Mexico the line of a "river" is clearly seen. Each line of scan is shown on the picture as parallel lines.

could fit into a medium-size toffee tin. With the use of satellites the pictures from Argo can be sent worldwide as they are actually seen underwater.

There is still a need for people to go to greater depths, despite the technological inventions. In 1989 the Japanese launched an undersea research vessel known as *Shinkai 6500* ("deep sea" in Japanese). It will dive deeper than any manned craft, to 7000 metres (about four miles). It weighs 25 tonnes, *carries* a crew of three and cruises at 2.5 knots. After trials it will start work in 1991.

To explore is one thing: to mine the ocean bed is another – as we shall see.

A side scan sonar picture of a sunken ship in the North Sea.

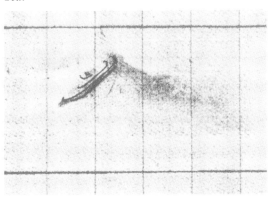

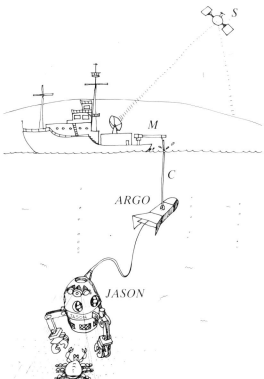

Argo *and* **Jason**.
A mother ship (M) cruises at a very slow speed with a stern cable linked to Argo. Argo has TV cameras and two sonar systems. Scientists on the ship look for items of interest and direct Jason to investigate. Jason has TV stereo cameras. Pictures from both Argo and Jason are beamed to a satellite (S), which transmits world wide what is actually being seen on the seabed.

Mining the Ocean Bed

Imagine a field of potatoes after the harvester has gone along the rows lifting the tubers from the ground, leaving the potatoes lying on the surface ready to be picked up. The potatoes will vary in size but generally all look alike, oval in shape and brown in colour. Imagine next a part of the ocean floor, deep down below the surface of the sea. Here you may see a "look-alike" scene to the potato field. Littering the floor there are not vegetables but hard rocky objects similar in sizes to the potatoes and similar, too, in shape and colour. If one of them is split open, like a baked potato ready for the butter or the cheese, an interesting pattern will be observed. You can see what I mean in the diagram.

An Iron Nodule similar to the seabed manganese nodules. The 50p piece gives you an idea of its size.

What we have is an agglomeration (bits joined together) of metallic pieces and other objects, to which is given the name NODULE. About half of each nodule is metal, made up of manganese and other elements, as the circle graph shows.

Nodules are not the only source of metals and other minerals on the ocean bottom. The first discovery of metal-rich muds in abundance was made in the Red Sea. Here they have accumulated in "deeps", which are depressions in the sea bed where the water temperature may exceed 55°C, due to local volcanic activity. Saudi Arabia and Sudan formed the Red Sea Commission in 1974 to exploit these muds. Preussag, a German company, have worked out a system to pump the muds to the surface from a depth of 2200 metres (about one-and-a-half miles), which will make commercial extraction possible before too long. Gold, too, is found in alluviam (sand and mud) under the sea, especially off Alaska, Australia and New Zealand.

Marine Polymetallic Sulphides (MPS) are mineral rich solid deposits firmly attached to the ocean bed, which occur in undersea volcanic areas. They contain up to twenty minerals in quantities which if they occurred on land it would start a mining rush! Preussag have designed electric grab dredge equipment to prize the MPSs from the seabed. To make it

Ocean areas with known deposits of deep sea Manganese Nodules.

financially worthwhile, the ore will have to be crushed and screened (sorted) below the ocean as well. Deposits of cobalt rich ores have been discovered firmly attached to the rocks underneath, like the crusts on loaves of bread. The costs involved in undersea mining are so great that at the present time it is far cheaper to mine land ores. Until land based metals become hard to find, and this is already happening with cobalt, it will not be worthwhile to mine the seas. Already Preussag have closed their undersea equipment manufacture.

The problems of mining the seabed are immense – the conservation factors are very serious as well and require far more research.

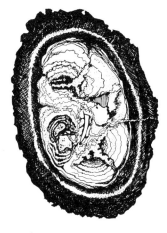

Cross section through a Manganese Nodule.
A thick outside skin surrounds a mass of smaller lumps of rock and metals stuck together around a "foreign body", such as a shark's tooth. The entire accumulation may take many million years to form.

Breaking up metallic ores from the seabed.
Recovered ores beside the **grappler**, *an electro-hydraulic grab with TV camera, which has been used to bring them to the surface.*

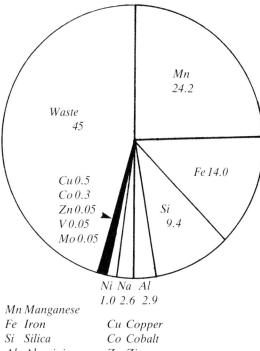

Mn Manganese
Fe Iron
Si   Silica   Cu Copper
Al   Aluminium   Co Cobalt
Na Sodium   Zn Zinc
Ni   Nickel   V   Vanadium
                         Mo Molybdenum

The percentage of minerals in Pacific Ocean nodules.
Source: J.L. Mero 1965.

We must be sure that the minerals are needed before environmental disturbance is wide-spread. Are we making the best use of recycled metals before we start to collect new ones from under the water?

Conservation considerations of undersea mining
1   Ore extraction will disturb the seabed with its plants and animals.
2   Unwanted waste will spread as a plume and "drown" the ocean bottom.
3   Disturbed sediment will muddy the water and stop light reaching plants and creatures.
4   Muddied water will prevent predators seeing their prey, or the prey seeing the predator.
5   Disturbing the bottom may release poison, chemicals or dumped waste.

Who owns these metallic fortunes? They occur in both the territorial waters of individual countries and, in by far the greatest quantities, in international waters. Is it, like fishing, a free-for-all with every country able to gather the rich harvest? The law of the sea is very complex.

Political Considerations

Until quite recent times the oceans of the world were taken to be a vast, boundless area of the world's surface which was free to all – the Freedom of the Seas. The only restricted part was the "territorial water" of each coastal country. This was a strip of sea three miles wide, the traditional maximum range of a cannon ball fired from the shore. In more recent times the width has been extended to 12 miles, and occasionally up to 200 miles.

With the discovery of mineral resources under the oceans and with the increase in the use of the seas for waste dumping the need for a set of rules has become apparent. In 1973 the Third Law of the Sea Conference began and went on, under the control of the United Nations, until 1982. The aim was to produce a set of rules concerning fisheries, navigation, continental shelves, the deep seabed, scientific research and pollution of the marine environment. One hundred and fifty nations failed to establish a world order beyond recognizing deep seabed as a "common heritage". One

hundred and thirtyfour nations signed the document, and this did NOT include the United Kingdom, the United States of America and West Germany. So far only 30 countries have ratified the treaty (accepted as part of their own laws), and 35 have rejected it. In fact the UK, USA, Belgium, West Germany, Italy, France, Japan and the USSR have agreed amongst themselves to licence deep-sea mining, which is directly against the UNCLOS III document (United Nations Conference on the Law Of the Sea).

UNCLOS III decisions.

40 per cent of the ocean is put under the control of coastal countries. There are four zones:

1. *Territorial Sea – complete control.*
2. *Contiguous Zone – limited control.*
3. *Extended Economic Zone (EEZ) – rights for economic activity (fishing, mining), scientific research, conservation.*
4. *Continental Shelf – exploration and exploitation permitted.*

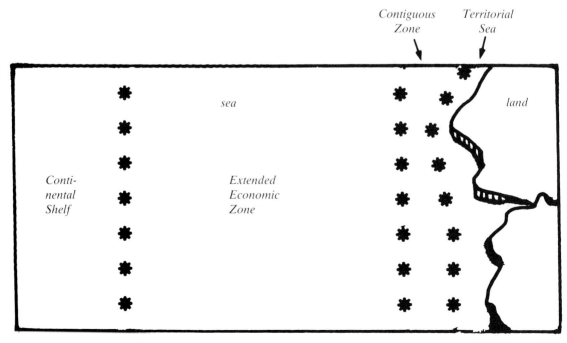

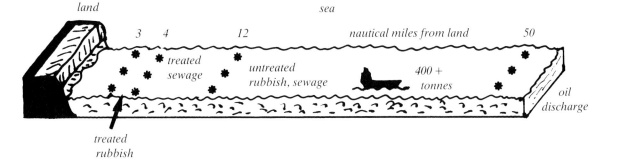

land · sea

3 4 12 nautical miles from land 50

treated sewage · untreated rubbish, sewage · 400 + tonnes · oil discharge

treated rubbish

MARPOL 1973. *The convention for the prevention of pollution from ships (MARitime POLlution) set rules for discharge from ships. The diagram shows how far from the shore it is permissible to dump various wastes into the sea. Ships over 400 tonnes must have tanks for waste oil.*

Some international progress has been made. The CCAMLR (Convention on the Conservation of Antarctica Marine Living Resources) has brought together some countries, including the UK, to control fishing in the Antarctic, particularly for krill. The IMO (International Maritime Organization) controls navigation and pollution from ships and the United Nations Environmental Programme has set up a regional seas programme to monitor the condition of specific areas of the seas. The ISA (International Seabed Authority) is the proposed body to control the exploitation of the deep seabed.

While the developed nations of the world see their future mineral resources lying on the seabed and while the developing nations wish not to be left out from these riches, the chances for international agreement seem a long way off.

Can you help?

Let us be sensible – there is little any of us can do to prevent the captains of ships flushing oil into the sea or their crews throwing rubbish over the side. We have little control over the way that sewage reaches the sea or that fertilizer from farms encourages the excessive growth of algae. Most of us live far away from the seashore and so cannot directly observe what is happening.

Yet, perhaps after all, we can help in our own small way – so that together with all the other people of the world we really make a difference, just as Jaques Cousteau realized. We could

use less electricity in our homes
travel by public transport (or walk the short distances)

recycle our waste
find out how our own sewage is treated and write to the water authority if we are not satisfied that it is being discharged into the river in a treated condition
take an active interest in our government's environmental plans and support those who try to improve them
join an "environmental" group such as a Watch Club (see glossary)
above all be interested in conservation matters

In all of these ways we could improve our contribution to the threat to the conditions of the oceans of the world.

Glossary

Aquaculture	Farming in water.
Bloom	High concentration of plankton.
Buoy	Floating object to aid navigation of ships.
Cod War	The name given to the dispute over fishing rights between Iceland and Britain.
Coelacanth	Deep sea fish "discovered" in 1952 when thought to be extinct.
Coelenterate	Jelly like animal, e.g. sea anemone, coral, jellyfish.
Coral reef	Rock in tropical water formed by the coral polyp.
Dredge	Collecting sediment from the river or seabed.
Dugong	Large seal like animal which lives only in fresh water.
Dune	Hill made of sand which is moved by the wind.
Estuary	Where a river joins the sea.
European Economic Community (EEC)	The affiliation of 12 European countries including the UK. Also known as The Common Market, with headquarters in Brussels.
Factory ship	Large ship to which fishing boats take their catch of fish to be processed.
Fathom	Unit of measurement of water depth. One fathom equals 1.83m or six feet.
Gill	The breathing organ of a fish either side of the head.
Greenpeace	Organization that tries to prevent environmental damage.
Habitat	Natural home of a plant or animal.
Ice Cap	The ice covering at the two poles, Arctic (north), Antarctic (south).
Knot	Measurement of speed on water. One knot is one nautical mile per hour.
Lloyds	The company which insures ships. It is based in London.
Longshore drift	Movement of pebbles, sand etc, along the shore by the waves.
Manatee	Similar to a dugong, but can live in fresh and sea water.
Mangrove	Tree which grows on tropical shores of rivers and seas.
Marram grass	Tough grass with very long roots which grows on sand dunes and prevents erosion.
Nautical mile	Measurement of distance at sea agreed internationally in 1852. It is related to the distance covered by one degree of arc on a great circle across the earth, a great circle being the shortest distance between two places on a sphere. One nautical mile equals 1.1508 land miles.
Nekton	The collective name for all animals which swim in the sea.
Nematocyst	Stinging cell of a coelenterate.
Oceania	Alternative name for the continent which includes Australia.
Ocean trench	Very deep "valley" in the seabed.
Photosynthesis	Process by which plants use sunlight to make food.
Plankton	Small plants (phytoplankton) and animals (zooplankton) which live in the top part of the sea.
Plimsoll line	Safety mark and line on sea going ships to prevent overloading. Named after Samuel Plimsoll, who suggested the scheme.
Radar	System of navigation which relies on an electrical impulse bouncing back to be displayed on a TV screen.
Sewage (raw)	Human waste usually flushed away down a toilet untreated sewage.
Sewage sludge	Solid waste that settles out of raw sewage by gravity.
(raw)	Untreated sewage sludge.
(digested)	Sludge that has been fermented until it decomposes.
(activated)	Digested sludge which has had a second fermentation and then dried. It is often sold in bags as dry fertilizer. Sludge from industrial urban areas contains zinc, copper, lead, chromium, nickel and cadmium. It is no use as a fertilizer.
Submersible	Underwater vessel in which the crew is kept at normal air pressure.
Tsunami	Enormous ocean wave caused by an undersea earthquake. It can swamp coastal areas and cause major damage.
Watch club	Groups for young people organized by the Watch Trust for Environmental Education, at The Green, Nettleham, Lincoln LN2 2NR. Regular newspaper, activities and information on the environment. Schools or others can form Watch Clubs.

Resources List

Magazines
National Geographic, Volume 160, No 6 December 1981

Books
The Gaia Atlas of Planet Management, Norman Myers, Pan Books, 1985
The Cousteau Almanac, Jaques-Yves Cousteau, Columbus Books, 1981
The Ocean World of Jaques Cousteau, Ed. Richard Murphy, Angus & Robertson
  (UK) 1975
Considering Conservation Series, Dryad Press
  Hunting Shooting and Fishing, Philip Neal 1987
  The Greenhouse Effect and Ozone Layer, Philip Neal 1989
  Energy, Power Sources and Electricity, Philip Neal, 1989
  The World's Water, Joy Palmer, 1987
  War on Waste, Joy Palmer, 1988
Oceans and Seas, T. Jennings, Oxford University Press
Atlas of the Sea around the British Isles, Ministry of Agriculture, Fisheries and
  Food, 1981
Harvest from the Sea, Oxfam, 1985 (Posters and teaching set)
Restless Oceans (Planet Earth series), A.B.C. Whipple, Time Life
The Oceans, David Lambert, Ward Lock, 1979

*Leather Back Turtle. Female turtles come ashore to
bury their eggs in the warm sand. This is not possible
if a building now occupies the beach or their night time
journey ashore is disturbed by barbecue and other
beach parties with people having a good but "turtle-
disturbing" time. In some places, Cyprus and
Malaysia for example, turtle reserves are established
in order to encourage these extraordinary creatures to
breed.*

Useful Addresses

British Antarctic Survey,
High Cross,
Madingley Road,
Cambridge CB3 0ET

Department of Agriculture,
   Fisheries and Food for Scotland,
Marine Laboratory,
PO Box 101,
Victoria Road,
Aberdeen AB9 8DB

Friends of the Earth,
26-28 Underwood Street,
London N1 7JQ

Greenpeace,
36 Graham Street,
London N1 8LL

Marine Conservation Society,
4 Gloucester Road,
Ross on Wye HR9 5BU

Marine Information and Advisory
   Service,
Deacon Laboratory,
Brook Road,
Wormley,
Godalming GU8 5UB

Ministry of Agriculture, Fisheries
   and Food,
Fisheries Laboratory,
Pakefield Road,
Lowestoft NR33 0HT

Nature Conservancy Council,
Northminster House,
Peterborough, PE1 1UA

Nuclear Industry Radioactive
   Waste Executive (NIREX),
Curie Avenue,
Harwell, OX11 0RA

Oxfam,
274 Banbury Road,
Oxford OX2 7DZ

Royal National Lifeboat
   Institution,
West Quay Road,
Poole, Dorset BH15 1HZ

Seafish Industry Authority,
144 Cromwell Road,
London SW7 4EF
and
10 Young Street,
Edinburgh EH2 4JQ

Shellfish Association of
   Great Britain,
Fishmongers' Hall,
London Bridge,
London EC4R 9EL

UK Atomic Energy Authority,
11 Charles II Street,
London SW1Y 4QP

United Nations Environment
   Programme,
PO Box 30552,
Nairobi,
Kenya

World Wide Fund for Nature,
Panda House,
11-13 Ockford Road,
Godalming,
Surrey GU7 1QU

Index

Acid Rain 44
Algae 41, 42, 60
Amazon 35
Ambergris 26
Antarctic 5, 10, 22, 23, 25, 52, 59
Aquaculture 20
Arctic 10, 27, 52
Argo and *Jason* 54, 55
Atlantic 14, 17, 24, 40, 46

Baleen 22
Baltic sea 47

Bathysphere 54
Bay of Fundy 12
Beach 6
Beachy Head 9
Bends 54
Blackpool 41
Bloom 42, 53
Blubber 30
Breakwater 10
Brighton 9

Carbon dioxide 14, 52, 53

Caribbean 4, 41
CCAMLR 59
Cephalopod 17, 24
CFC 52
Chesapeake Bay 43
Clam 50
Coastguards 8
Cod War 16
Coelacanth 29
Contiguous Zone 58
Continental Shelf 58
Copepod 15

Coral Reef 7
Corinth Canal 8
Coriolis Effect 11
Cousteau, Jaques 31, 54, 60

DDT 10, 15
Dead Sea 51
Demersal 16, 18
Detergent 37, 39
Dioxin 35, 45
Dolphin 26, 30, 31
Dolphinarium 30
Drift net 17

Eastbourne 7
EEC 40, 43
Ekman flow 11
English Channel 8, 35
Estuary 12
Euphausiid 22
Extended Economic Zone 58
Exxon Valdez 10, 38, 39

Falkland Islands 24, 25
Faroes Grind 27
Fertilizer 34, 40, 60
Fibre optic 54
Fish farm 20, 21
Fishing, industrial 16, 17, 18
Flag of convenience 9
Flotsam 11
Food chain 15
    web 28

Gaff 16
GLORIA 54, 55
Greenhouse Effect 14, 44, 52, 53
Greenpeace 45, 46
Gulf of Mexico 4, 36
Gulf Stream Drift 5, 11, 14, 51

Hastings 8, 9, 36
Herald of Free Enterprise 9
Holidays 6, 7
Hydraulic Grab 57
Hypertrophication 20, 42

IMO 59
Incineration 45
International Whaling Commission 27
Irish Sea 46
ISA 59
Ixtoc 1 36

Jack Sail by the Wind 32
Jig 24
Jellyfish 15, 32, 33
Jojoba 27

Kelp 21
Krill 22, 23, 28, 59

Lateen sail 32
Law of the sea 58
Leukaemia 46

Lindisfarne 7
Lighthouse 9
Lightship 8
Lipid microlayer 45
Lloyds 9
London 52
    Dumping Convention 45
Longshore drift 10

Manganese 56, 57
Mangrove 7
Marine incineration 44
Marpol 59
Marram grass 6
Mediterranean Sea 4, 6, 8, 12, 37, 41
Mercury 35
Mermaid 28
Methane 52
Minamata Bay 35
Mining 56
MPS 56

Nature reserve 6, 7
Narwhal 26, 31
Navigation 8
Nematocyst 32, 33
New York 42, 43, 52
Nodule 56, 57
North Sea 4, 20, 35, 36, 42, 45, 55
    Conference 45
Norway 48
Nuclear waste 34, 46, 47
Nuvan 20

Ocean current 4, 5, 10, 11, 14, 38, 48
    turbine 51
Ocean water cooling 49
Octopus 25, 33
Oil 36, 37, 38, 59, 60
    discharge 8, 10
    pollution 36, 37, 38, 39
    sea birds 37
    skimmers 37
    sludge 37
Open coast barrage 50, 51
Oscillating water column 49
Oscillating vane 50
OTEC 49, 51
Outfall 40, 41
Oxygen 14, 42
Ozone layer 53

Pacific 4, 17, 24, 30, 38, 40
Panama canal 8
PCB 15, 44
Pelagic 16
Piper Alpha 35, 36
Plankton 14, 15, 16, 22, 28, 45, 53
Plimsoll 59
Pollution 8, 10, 12, 35, 45, 59
Porpoise 17, 31
Portuguese Man-of-War 32, 33
Purse seine 18, 19

Raft 50

Rance tidal power 48
Rectifier lock 50
Red Sea 56
Roll-on, roll-off 8
Royal National Lifeboat Institution 3
Royal Sovereign 8
RSPCA 37

Saline power 49, 51
Salmon 20, 39
Sand dune 6
San Francisco 46
Sargasso Sea 11
Saundersfoot 12
Scuba 54
Sea bathing 7
Sea level 52
Seal 35
Sediment 34, 57
Seine net 18
Sellafield 46
Severn 12, 50
Sewage 6, 34, 35, 40, 41, 42, 43, 52, 59,
    60
Shark 16, 30
Shellfish 16, 17, 20, 21, 23, 28, 42
Shrimp 17, 21, 22, 23
Sonar scan 54
Southampton 12
Spermaceti oil 26, 27
Squid 15, 17, 22, 24, 26
SSSI 50
Starfish 25
St Lawrence 15
Suez canal 8
Sweden 47

Tapchan Power 48
Tar ball 37
Tentacle 32, 33
Territorial water 57, 58
Thames 42, 52, 53
Tide 10, 12, 13, 42, 48, 51
    mill 48
    power 50, 51
Torrey Canyon 37, 39
Tourism 7
Trawl 18, 19
Trinity Hose 8
Turtle 6, 7, 17, 33

UK Nirex 47
UNCLOS 58
UNEP 59

Vitrify 47

Water cycle 5
Waves 58
Weather forecast areas 5
Whalebone 26
Whales 17, 21, 22, 23, 24, 26, 27, 28, 38
WHO 54
Wind power 51